TIME TO CHOOSE

A GRASSROOTS STUDY GUIDE ON THE NUCLEAR ARMS RACE FROM A CHRISTIAN PERSPECTIVE

Celebration

First published 1983

© Celebration Services (Post Green) Ltd. 1983

British Library Cataloguing in Publication Data
Time to Choose
1. Atomic weapons and disarmament
2. War and religion
I. Barker, Martha Keys   II. Nobbs, Val
261.8'73   JX1974.7

ISBN 0-906309-24-7

Designed by: Peter Lusby Taylor

Photoset by: Furlonger Phototext Ltd., Bournemouth.

*Printed and bound in Great Britain for Celebration
Services (Post Green) Ltd., 57 Dorchester Road,
Lytchett Minster, Poole, Dorset BH16 6JE by Bourne
Press Ltd., Bournemouth*

About the Authors

Martha Keys Barker was born in New Jersey, USA. She received her B.A. in sociology from Rice University in Houston, Texas. After three years of involvement in the ministry of the Church of the Redeemer in Houston she joined *The Fisherfolk*, a travelling group which uses music and the performing arts to encourage church renewal. Invited to England in 1972, The Fisherfolk travelled extensively in England, Scotland, Sweden and Germany. She has co-authored two books concerning the use of the arts in church renewal – *The Folk Arts in Renewal* and *Building Worship Together*. She is a member of the Community of Celebration on the Isle of Cumbrae, Scotland.

Alan Kreider was born in Indiana, USA. He received his B.A. from Goshen College and his M.A. and Ph.D. from Harvard University. His research and writing includes English Reformation history, the history of the Radical Reformation and of the Early Church and the history and theology of Christian approaches to war and peace. He is co-convenor of the Shaftesbury Project Study Group on War and Peace, co-pastor of the London Mennonite Fellowship and director of the London Mennonite Resource Centre. He lives in community with 25 people in Highgate, London.

Val Nobbs was born in Ilford, Essex. She graduated from Warwick University with a B.A.

honours in English and European literature. For the past 9 years she has lived in the Community of Celebration, a Christian life-style community whose members are radically committed to be a sign of celebration of life in Jesus Christ and a friend of the poor and oppressed. She is the editor of Faith Lees' recent book *Break Open My World* and currently resides with the community on the Isle of Cumbrae, Scotland.

Donald Scott is Scottish. He received an Honours B.Sc. in Mathematics from Edinburgh University. He has worked as a teacher and a social worker and lives in Edinburgh.

Mike Sweatman was born in Karachi of British parents. He studied metallurgy and now works in Recycles – a bicycle co-operative in Edinburgh.

GrassRoots Magazine

GrassRoots Magazine seeks to explore what it means for the church to be the people of God, making specific the principles of the kingdom and praying and working for unity, healing and reconciliation in the world. It is published bi-monthly by Celebration.

Time to Choose is the first study guide to appear in conjunction with the magazine. News and articles on the nuclear arms race from a Christian perspective and on paths to peacemaking are a regular feature of the magazine.

Acknowledgements

The editors wish to thank many of the artists and publishers who have contributed their work without charge to this book.

The authors gratefully acknowledge the use of the following material:

Extracts and Articles

Extracts from *Hiroshima*, by John Hersey, copyright 1946 and renewed 1974 by John Hersey. Reprinted by permission of Alfred A. Knopf, Inc. Originally appeared in *The New Yorker*.

Articles reprinted from *Sojourners* Magazine, PO Box 29272, Washington DC 20017. Used with permission.

Photographs and Illustrations

Ash and Grant: 23, 26, 41

Ashmolean Museum, Oxford, 58, 61

Campaign Against Arms Trade: 108

Central Office of Information: 33

Duccio: 75

Japan Information Centre: 15, 17, 18, 22

Kathe Kollwitz, Germany; Elefanten Press, Writers & Readers Publishing Cooperative – Pantheon Edition: 39, 111, 113

Peter Lusby Taylor: 24, 28, 34, 41, 43, 62, 63, 65, 70, 81, 83, 84, 86, 87, 105, 106, 117

Mary Rose Trust: 61 (bottom)

Morag MacDougall, photographed by Chris Hill and Lesley Reid: 92, 93, 94, 95

Len Munnik, Holland: 10, 12, 50, 51, 78, 96

Paul Peter Piech, BFA, FSTD: 44, 47, 48, 115

Sojourners: Todd Mayforth, 40; Buu Chi, 72; Dan Hubig, 118; others: 43 (top) 55, 69, 77, 97, 98, 120

The Tablet: 56

US Navy: 35, 103

Contents

Introduction

In late 1980, when we began to think about producing this study guide, we were concerned about the lack of public awareness of the issues raised by the nuclear arms race. Since that time, however, there has been a marked upsurge in both public awareness and media coverage. For Christians, the issue of nuclear war is emerging as one which must be considered anew from a biblical and theological perspective. The leaders of many churches have made statements calling for urgent reassessment of our present dependence on nuclear weapons.

Though there has been an increase in media coverage on the issue, it is easy for individuals to feel bewildered and overwhelmed by conflicting opinions and to be left feeling powerless in the face of forces beyond their control. This guide is designed for group study, in the hope that within a group, individuals may find an arena to explore some of the basic facts about nuclear weapons, to examine their attitudes, to express their concerns, and to determine their future actions in response to these issues.

The contributors to the course are united in the conviction that reliance on nuclear weapons is not a political question to be left to 'experts' but one with which each person must struggle as a matter of faith, as a matter of humanity. This course is the fruit of our struggle to understand the issues raised by nuclear armaments and to find ways to respond faithfully.

The study guide is divided into three parts. In the first, we look at the nature of nuclear weapons and nuclear war, the arms race and Britain's defence policy. In the second, we consider war from a biblical and theological perspective. We examine the traditional Christian attitudes of 'the just war' and pacifism and evaluate them in the light of Old and New Testament teachings. The final section is concerned with responses to the issues raised in the first two sections. In it we reflect on personal pilgrimages in peacemaking,

and suggest possibilities for action. We also consider the central place of prayer and worship in peacemaking, and provide materials on these themes for use in worship events. A reference section lists organisations for further involvement and suggests resources for continuing study.

How to Use the Study Guide

The course is designed for use by groups: church groups, bible study groups, house groups, inter-church study groups: if desired, it may also be used for individual study. It is divided into 12 sessions, each of which lasts for 1½-2 hours. There should be a week or a fortnight between sessions to allow for preparation. At the end of each session are questions for study and discussion. Some are designed for individual study – to review the main points of the section, to help to remember and articulate them; other questions are designed to stimulate individual response to the section and to promote group discussion. Individuals may also formulate their own questions which are raised by the material and use these as a basis for group discussion.

In preparation for the session each person should read through the material and think through the questions, perhaps making brief notes. In some cases more questions are given than can be covered in one session. The group should select beforehand the particular questions they would like to discuss for the next session. When the group meets, one member should begin with a summary of the main points of the reading. If a large group is doing the course, it should be sub-divided into smaller discussion groups of 5-7 members to allow enough time for individuals to express their ideas. The discussion should then cover either the set questions, or others which are raised in the group.

We would emphasise the importance of free-

dom in the discussion. The purpose of discussion is not to come to a conclusion, but to give individuals opportunity to examine their feelings, ideas and convictions, and to hear and understand the position of others. In discussion we would encourage members of the group to seek to understand the positions of others, rather than defending their own position. Attempts should not be made to 'convince others' but rather to understand and remain in dialogue. Similarly, in such discussion it is not uncommon to realise that we hold conflicting views within ourselves – we may think one thing, but have conflicting feelings. It is our hope that the group could be a place to share such internal conflicts and to give time and attention to them. Finally, groups may find it encouraging to spend some time in each session in prayer since discussion of these issues is not theoretical, but addresses us at the level of our fears, our faith and our commitment.

PART
I

The Nuclear Option

Introduction to Part One

It is the nature of the nuclear weapons issue that the 'facts' are not necessarily agreed upon by all concerned. As a result, some of the information we present is widely agreed upon while some is more controversial.

Our purpose is to question the current policy of reliance on nuclear weapons and to suggest that other policies do exist. It is perhaps significant to note that in all our reading we found a scarcity of material on alternative defence policy. This may partly be due to the fact that the nuclear option has so dominated post-war defence planning that other options have been neglected. Recently, as the commitment to nuclear weapons is increasingly being questioned, other possibilities are being more widely considered. It is our hope that this study might foster discussion of alternatives where until recently there has been a quiet acceptance of things as they are.

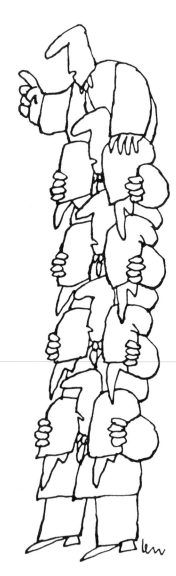

A Nuclear Attack on Britain

In 1980 the British Government carried out an exercise to test out its preparations for a nuclear attack. 'Operation Squareleg', as this simulation of nuclear war was called, is used as a rough basis for the narrative that follows.[1]

The quotes are from Hiroshima *by John Hersey.[2] John Hersey was sent to Hiroshima nine months after the atomic bomb exploded and based his book on the experiences of six survivors of the explosion.*

The Haig family live in a village a few miles outside an industrial city in Britain. They become aware of an international crisis some months before the attack (scheduled for 19 September 1980) but do not get a true impression of the seriousness of the situation as government sources play down the threat in the hope of negotiating a solution to the crisis. The government is particularly unwilling to make overt preparation for an attack for fear of antagonising the enemy.

By 27 August the government considers the threat serious enough to remove art treasures to their special bunker. By now the tension in the country breaks out; on 31 August there is 'industrial arrest (sic) and large scale activity by extreme left and right wing parties'.[3] Troops are called in to deal with anti-war demonstrations in Stafford and the West Midlands.

On 13 September panic buying starts in the cities and despite government pressure to stay at home, 'those living on high rise flats and in areas generally thought to be obvious targets leave home quickly'.[4]

In Warwickshire the population increases by 200,000 (about 50%) as evacuees flood out of Birmingham. War is declared on 15 September and the government moves to its many bunkers dotted around the country. However, pressure is stepped up to stop people evacuating the cities. Most main roads are designated 'Essential Service Routes' for use by the military only, and the government exercises its policy of not supplying evacuees with accommodation, food or other essentials.

The Haig family, feeling far enough from a major target, do not move out to the country. When war is declared they take a few precautions – they whitewash and tape the windows, fill all available containers with water and barricade windows and doors of an inner room with furniture. In this room they place all the items that the government advise them to have – radios, packs of cards, and the like.

In the first few days of war there are a number of conventional bombing raids and more and more people try to leave the cities, completely blocking the minor roads that are not under military control.

The first nuclear attack lasts from 12 noon to 12.10 Friday 19 September. The second strike lasts from 1 p.m. to 3 p.m.

'At exactly fifteen minutes past eight in the morning on 6 August 1945, Japanese time ... the atomic bomb flashed over Hiroshima ... As Mrs Nakamura stood watching her neighbour, everything flashed whiter than any white she had ever seen. She did not notice what happened to the man next door; the reflex of a mother set her in motion towards her children. She had taken a single step ... when something picked her up and she seemed to fly into the next room ... pursued by parts of her house.

Timbers fell around her as she landed, and a shower of tiles pommelled her; everything became dark, for she was buried. The debris did not cover her deeply. She rose up and freed herself. She heard a child cry, "Mother, help me!" and saw her youngest – Myeko, the five-year-old – buried up to her breast and unable to move. As Mrs Nakamura started frantically to claw her way towards the baby, she could see or hear nothing of her other children.'[5]

13

By lunch time over one hundred nuclear weapons have struck targets in the UK. Half as many weapons again have been launched but a significant number have failed to reach their targets. The targets chosen range from British and American nuclear weapon bases through strategic targets, such as airfields, ports, depots, communication, command and control centres, to urban industrial centres.

Surprisingly London is not a target per se although much of the capital is destroyed by bombs aimed at specific targets around it. A huge five megaton* bomb in the Thames estuary between Canvey Island and Chatham not only destroys the nearby refinery and naval base, it also floods London. There are also some sinister targets – a groundburst at Eastbourne covers south London with fallout, while a groundburst on the Windscale nuclear plant (containing stored civil nuclear waste) covers much of south Scotland with fallout.

Among the military targets US bases take clear prominence with a wide range of bases attacked.

A 150 kiloton* warhead is detonated above the industrial sector of the city six miles from the Haig family's house. The bomb completely obliterates everything within one mile of 'ground-zero' – the point immediately below the centre of the explosion. At two miles from ground-zero most buildings are destroyed, all trees are blown down, there are 190 m.p.h. winds, many buildings are on fire.

Four miles from ground-zero winds reach 60 m.p.h.; all windows are broken, causing injuries from flying glass and debris, many buildings are moderately damaged and people directly exposed to the explosion suffer burns.

'The morning (after the day of the explosion) again, was hot. Father Kleinsorge went to fetch water for the wounded in a bottle and a teapot he had borrowed ... On his way back with the water ... he heard a voice ask from the underbrush, "Have you got anything to drink?" He saw a uniform. Thinking there was just one soldier, he approached with the water. When he had penetrated the bushes, he saw there were about twenty men, and they were all in exactly the same nightmarish state: their faces were wholly burned, their eyesockets were hollow, the fluid from their melted eyes had run down their cheeks.

(They must have had their faces upturned when the bomb went off; perhaps they were anti-aircraft personnel.) Their mouths were mere swollen, pus-covered wounds, which they could not bear to stretch enough to admit the spout of the teapot. So Father Kleinsorge got a large piece of grass and drew out the stem so as to make a straw, and gave them all water to drink that way.

Since that day, Father Kleinsorge has thought back to how queasy he had once been at the sight of pain ... Yet there in the park he was so benumbed that immediately after leaving this horrible sight he stopped on a path by one of the pools and discussed with a lightly wounded man whether it would be safe to eat the fat, two-foot carp that floated dead on the surface of the water. They decided, after some consideration, that it would be unwise.'[6]

At the first warning of attack the Haig family retires to their prepared room. They experience the nearby explosion as a flash followed twenty seconds later by a blast wave like a combination of an earthquake and a hurricane. The blast wave shatters all the windows in the house and demolishes some of the houses in the area. Anybody outside, and many people inside buildings, are injured by flying debris, glass, roof tiles, tree branches or by falling masonry. Some houses in the area catch fire.

'Mr Tanimoto, fearful for his family and church, at first ran towards them by the shortest route, along Koi highway. He was the only person making his way into the city; he met hundreds and hundreds who were fleeing, and every one of them seemed to be hurt in some way. The eyebrows of some were burned off and skin hung from their faces and hands ... Some were vomiting as they walked. Many were naked or in shreds of clothing. On some undressed bodies, the burns had made patterns – ... on the skin of some women, the shapes of flowers they had had on their kimonos. Many, although injured themselves, supported relatives who were worse off. Almost all had their heads bowed, looked straight ahead, were silent, and showed no expression whatever.

After crossing Koi bridge and Kannon bridge, having run the whole way, Mr Tanimoto saw, as he approached the centre, that all the houses had been crushed and many were afire. Here the trees

* see glossary, p.116

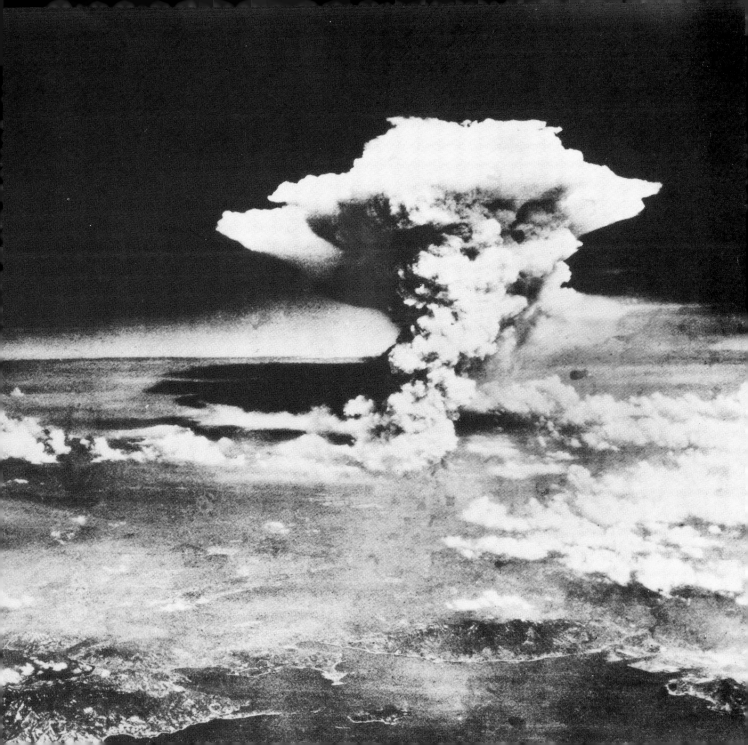

were bare and their trunks were charred. He tried at several points to penetrate the ruins, but the flames always stopped him. Under many houses, people screamed for help, but no one helped; in general, survivors that day assisted only their relatives or immediate neighbours ...'[7]

If they survived the blast wave the Haig family would not rush outside to help their friends and neighbours; they would stay in their sanctuary room, sealing it as best they could, to keep out radioactive fallout. The fallout from the airburst described above would consist of a very fine dust formed from radioactive fission products and bomb materials intimately mixed together. This dust would be so light that it would rise high into the atmosphere and would not fall close to the initial explosion. The chances are that the Haig's home would be in an area that would be exposed to fallout from groundbursts on military targets in that part of the country. These groundbursts, being on key military targets, would be likely to happen early in the attack and so fallout might become a real danger even before the bomb near the Haig's home exploded. The dangers from fallout are very difficult to predict as it is blown in the direction of the prevailing wind and is 'washed' out of the sky by rainfall. However, the concentration of targets listed in the Squareleg operation is so high that most of the country would be exposed to some fallout in almost all types of weather.

The Haigs would desperately need information on what had happened and how to keep themselves alive, but with no British TV or radio stations able to broadcast and no mains electricity or operating telephones they would probably have to rely on short wave broadcasts from overseas; after a few days domestic radio broadcasts would start again. Lacking information on local radiation, the Haig family would have to stay in their sanctuary room for a full two weeks to be confident that they had avoided the most serious effects of fallout. Knowing that the hazard was greatest during the first two days the parents might forbid anybody to leave the room for forty-eight hours. They would all have to use the improvised toilet placed near the door. They would also ignore the desperate attempts of those whose houses had been destroyed, to find a fallout room in which to shelter. Anyone who had been outside a couple of hours after the attack would be dangerously contaminated with radioactive fallout. After two days adults would leave the room for a few seconds at a time to empty the toilet bucket. Although children might initially enjoy the novelty of the situation, as time wore on the increasing boredom, stale air and fetid conditions would rapidly strain everyone's patience. Towards the end of the two weeks food and water would be getting short and the state of the room would be intolerably unhygienic. The pressure to leave the shelter would become unbearable especially as the two week deadline seems so artificial. Towards the end of the shelter period adults who had left the shelter to empty the toilet bucket might start to show symptoms of radiation sickness. It would be difficult for others in the shelter to know if this were genuine radiation sickness or simply the effects of the strain of living in the shelter.

'Dr Sasaki and his colleagues at the Red Cross Hospital watched the unprecedented disease unfold and at last evolved a theory about its nature. It had, they decided, three stages. The first stage ... was the direct reaction to the bombardment of the body, at the moment when the bomb went off, by neutrons, beta particles, and gamma rays. The apparently uninjured people who had died so mysteriously in the first few hours or days had succumbed in this first stage. The rays simply destroyed body cells ... Many people who did not die right away came down with nausea, headache, diarrhoea, malaise, and fever, which lasted several days. Doctors could not be certain whether some of these symptoms were the result of radiation or nervous shock. The second stage set in 10 or 15 days after the bombing. The main symptom was falling hair. Diarrhoea and fever, which in some cases went as high as 106, came next. Twenty-five to thirty days after the explosion blood disorders appeared: gums bled, the white-blood-cell count dropped sharply and petechiae (haemorrhages about the size of grains of rice) appeared on the skin and mucous membranes. The drop in the number of white blood corpuscles reduced the patient's capacity to resist infection, so open wounds were unusually slow in healing and many of the sick developed sore throats and mouths. Towards the end of the second stage, if the patient survived, anaemia, or a drop in the red blood count, also set in. The third stage was the reaction that came

16

Sculpture commemorating the atomic explosion at Hiroshima.

Overleaf
The aftermath of the explosion showing the Sangyō Shōrei-kan (Hiroshima Industrial Production hall). It is nowadays called the Atomic Dome and has become the symbol of Hiroshima.

Facing page 14
The world's first uranium bomb dropped on Hiroshima, August 6th 1945. This aerial photograph was taken about one hour after the bomb was dropped, at about 80km from Hiroshima.

when the body struggled to compensate for its ills – when, for instance, the white count not only returned to normal but increased to much higher than normal levels. In this stage, many patients died of complications, such as infections in the chest cavity. Most burns healed with deep layers of pink, rubbery scar tissue, known as keloid tumours. The duration of the disease varied, depending on the patient's constitution and the amount of radiation he had received. Some victims recovered in a week; with others the disease dragged on for months.'[8]

Living in the shelter room would be particularly difficult for the old and those who were not well at the time of the attack. Exposure to any radiation lowers the body's capacity to fight the infection that fetid conditions would encourage. In all likelihood, at least one person in the Haig family would die while in the fallout shelter. The government anticipates this and gives the following instructions:

'. . . place the body in another room and cover it as securely as possible. Attach an identification. You should receive radio instructions on what to do next. If no instructions have been given within five days, you should temporarily bury the body as soon as it is safe to go out, and mark the spot.'[9]

To survive the attack, as most of the Haig family did, would be exceptional. Most people in and around the target area would be dead or seriously wounded. There would be massive destruction by blast and fire and those who did survive would be left without any means of protecting themselves from fallout. While the nuclear planners can tell us that a certain blast is fatal and a certain level of radiation is likely to cause death, no one really knows what the combined effect of all these factors would be. Certainly many more people would die from a combination of effects, none of which would be lethal by itself.

After a major attack on Britain the services on which the community relies would simply not exist. Health services, fire services, the police, food and fuel supply, are all controlled from the city centres and would be effectively destroyed in an attack.

'Of a hundred and fifty doctors in the city, sixty-five were already dead and most of the rest were wounded. Of 1,780 nurses, 1,654 were dead or too badly hurt to work ... the sole uninjured doctor on the Red Cross Hospital staff was Dr Sasaki ... In a city of two hundred and forty-five thousand, nearly a hundred thousand people had been killed or doomed at one blow; a hundred thousand more were hurt. At least ten thousand of the wounded made their way to the best hospital in town, (the Red Cross Hospital).'[10]

Only those who could manage entirely without help from others would survive. Conditions after an attack would be ripe for a complete breakdown of law and order. There would be a large number of people desperate for food, water and shelter, and those who were not desperately in need would be living in fear of radiation – and trying to defend their shelter space. this has led many people to suggest that society would revert to tribal savagery. The experience of Hiroshima and Nagasaki, however, would seem to be that the shock of the attack, rather than turning people into self-interested savages, makes them completely apathetic, completely uninterested in saving themselves from the simplest dangers. There is no way of predicting what would happen after an attack except that it would contain elements of both those responses.

'A year after the bomb was dropped, Miss Sasaki was a cripple; Mrs Nakamura was destitute; Father Kleinsorge was back in the hospital; Dr Sasaki was not capable of the work he once could do; Mr Tanimoto's church had been ruined and he no longer had his exceptional vitality. The lives of these six people, who were among the luckiest in Hiroshima, would never be the same.'[11]

On finally leaving their shelter, the Haig family would emerge into a country where up to three quarters of the population had been killed, where the complex social network required to support industry had been shattered, where farms – unused to providing directly for local needs and badly hit by fallout – could not feed even the tiny population remaining, and where the survivors of the attack could look forward to a winter spent in damaged housing without adequate fuel supplies.

Moreover, it would not be a question of putting up with these problems for a few months. A major attack on Britain would be likely to be part of a world war that included major nuclear attacks on much of Europe, the USA and Russia. Such a war

The Memorial Park, Hiroshima.

would totally destroy the world's economy, there would be no nation on earth that would be in any position to supply the kind of aid that the USA supplied to the countries of western Europe after the Second World War. The Haig family would be largely fending for themselves, living in a pre-industrial society not just for a winter but for at least a decade and maybe considerably longer.

'A surprising number of the people of Hiroshima remained more or less indifferent about the ethics of using the bomb. Possibly they were too terrified by it to want to think about it at all . . . As for the use of the bomb, she (Mrs Nakamura) would say, "It was war and we had to expect it." And then she would add, "Shikata ga nai" . . . "It can't be helped. Oh, well. Too bad."

Many citizens of Hiroshima, however, continued to feel a hatred for Americans which nothing could possibly erase. "I see," Dr Sasaki once said, "that they are holding a trial for war crimi- *nals in Tokyo just now. I think they ought to try the men who decided to use the bomb and they should hang them all."*[12]

Notes: A Nuclear Attack on Britain

1. Duncan Campbell, 'World War III: An Exclusive Preview', in *Britain and the Bomb: The New Statesman papers on defence and disarmament* (New Statesman, 1981), 65-70.
2. John Hersey, *Hiroshima* (Penguin, 1946).
3. Duncan Campbell, 'In Place of Civil Defence', in *Britain and the Bomb*, 76.
4. Ibid.
5. Hersey, *Hiroshima*.
6. Ibid.
7. Ibid.
8. Ibid.
9. Central Office of Information, prepared for the Home Office, *Protect and Survive* (H.M.S.O., 1980), 24.
10. Hersey, *Hiroshima*.
11. Ibid.
12. Ibid.

Weapon Effects

This section describes the effect of a nuclear explosion on an urban area. It is a resumé of a study of the effects of nuclear war by the US Congress Office of Technology Assessment.[1] The introduction to the study states that the effects of such a blast which cannot be calculated are at least as important as those for which calculations are attempted. It also specifies that details of the effects would vary according to several factors: weapon design, the exact geographical layout of the target area, the materials and methods used for construction in the target area, and the weather.

The energy of a nuclear explosion is released in five different ways.

1. An explosive blast
2. Direct nuclear radiation
3. Direct thermal radiation mostly in the form of visible light
4. Pulses of electrical and magnetic energy called electromagnetic pulse (EMP)
5. The creation of a variety of radioactive particles which are thrown up in the air by the force of the blast and return to earth as radioactive fallout

The distribution of the bomb's energy among these effects depends on its size and design, however some generalisations are possible.

1. **Blast** – Most damage to cities from large weapons is from the explosive blast. The blast creates two effects: sudden changes in air pressure (called 'static overpressure') that crush objects, and high winds. In general large buildings are destroyed by the overpressure, while people and objects, such as trees, are destroyed by wind. The magnitude of the blast and its effect diminishes with the distance from the centre of the explosion. It is also related in a more complicated way to the height of the burst above ground level. A burst at ground level produces the greatest overpressure at very close ranges, but less overpressure than an airburst at somewhat longer range. This is why groundbursts are used to attack very hard, very small targets such as missile silos. An airburst might be used to attack factories or cities.

A typical groundburst digs out a large crater, depositing some of the materials around its rim, while the rest is carried up into the air and returns to earth as radioactive fallout. An airburst does not dig a crater and produces negligible immediate fallout.

Most blast deaths result from the collapse of buildings, from people being blown into objects, or from buildings or smaller objects being blown onto or into people. It is thus difficult to give precise information on how many people would be killed.

2. **Direct Nuclear Radiation** – Direct radiation occurs at the time of the explosion; it can be very intense but is short range. For large nuclear weapons, the range of intense direct radiation is less than the range of lethal blast. However, in the case of smaller weapons, such as those used in Japan in 1945, direct radiation may have a larger range than the lethal blast. In the short term a large dose of direct radiation (more than 50 rem*) gives rise to radiation sickness and half the people exposed to 450 rem are likely to die from this cause. In the long term even small doses can result in significant increases in the cancer rate, and in the occurrence of genetic defects. It should be clearly understood that a large nuclear war would expose the survivors, however well sheltered, to levels of radiation far greater than those considered safe in peacetime.

3. **Thermal Radiation** – A nuclear explosion gives rise to an intense blast of thermal radiation, i.e. heat and light which, as it travels at the speed of light, precedes the blast wave. This radiation can temporarily blind people and more seriously can burn people. A one megaton explosion can cause first degree burns (equivalent to

* see glossary, p.116

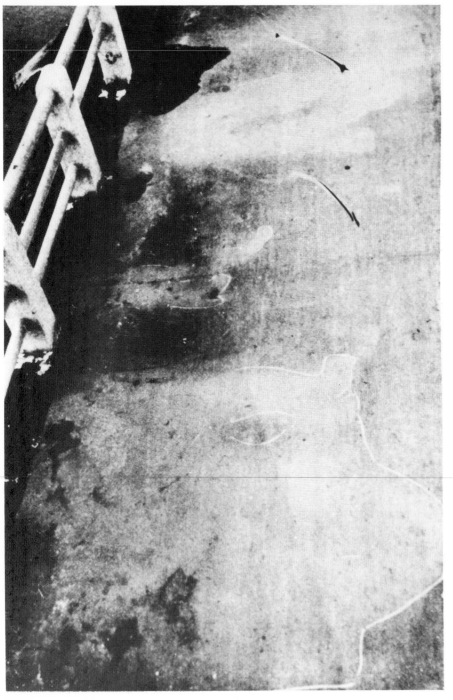

bad sunburn) at distances of about seven miles, second degree burns (producing blisters that lead to infection if untreated) at six miles, and third degree burns (which destroy skin tissue) at about five miles. Third degree burns over 24% of the body or second degree burns over 30% of the body will probably prove fatal with the lack of medical care available after a nuclear attack.

The distance at which dangerous burns occur depends on the weather (fog, etc.) and whether or not people are in the shadow of buildings.

Thermal radiation can also directly set buildings on fire and although the blast may 'blow out' some of these fires, it may also contribute to the fire hazard by damaging gas mains, boilers, fuel tanks and electrical circuits. It is then possible especially in denser cities, that these fires would coalesce into a firestorm or conflagration that would devastate areas of a city, and kill a high proportion of the people in the affected area.

4. **Electromagnetic Pulse** – The electromagnetic pulse is like a very strong pulse of radio waves and is not a physical threat to human beings. It does however affect computers, power lines and radio stations, although it is unlikely to damage a portable transistor radio.

5. **Fallout** a) *Airbursts*. While all nuclear explosions in the atmosphere produce some fallout the fallout threat from an airburst is trivial compared to its other consequences.

b) *Groundbursts*. The significant hazards come from particles scooped up from the ground. The radioactive particles that rise only a short distance will fall back to earth within minutes, landing close to ground-zero. In these areas most people will have already been killed, and so the fallout is unlikely to cause many more deaths.

The particles that rise higher will be carried some distance by the wind. The area and intensity of fallout is strongly influenced by local weather conditions. However, as a general rule the effect of fallout from a one megaton ground burst on people living outside shelters would be fatal. Furthermore, it would be about a decade before the radiation level outside the area of blast damage fell to the level considered safe in peace time. One particularly dangerous source of fallout would be a nuclear weapon destroying a nuclear power plant. Fallout from a destroyed nuclear reactor (whose destruction would require a very accurate groundburst) would not initially

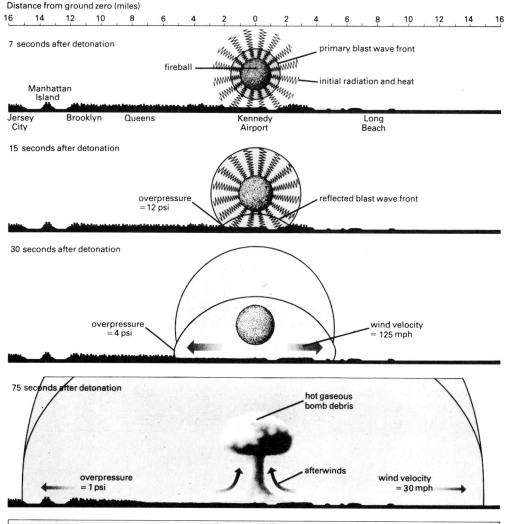

Distance from ground zero (miles)

16 14 12 10 8 6 4 2 0 2 4 6 8 10 12 14 16

7 seconds after detonation

primary blast wave front

fireball

initial radiation and heat

Manhattan Island

Jersey City   Brooklyn   Queens   Kennedy Airport   Long Beach

15 seconds after detonation

overpressure = 12 psi

reflected blast wave front

30 seconds after detonation

overpressure = 4 psi

wind velocity = 125 mph

75 seconds after detonation

hot gaseous bomb debris

overpressure = 1 psi

afterwinds

wind velocity = 30 mph

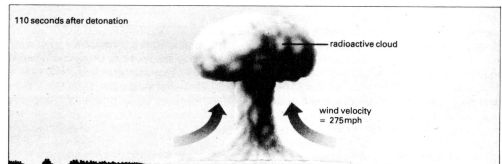

110 seconds after detonation

radioactive cloud

wind velocity = 275 mph

Diagram showing the effect of a 1-Mt weapon, airburst at 10,000 feet over New York City.

(opposite) 'Shadows' imprinted on the asphalt surface on the Mantai-bashi Bridge about 850 metres from the hypocentre. These are of a human figure pulling a cart. The larger area outlined in chalk is the 'shadow' of the cart, and the smaller area is that of the figure. These 'shadows' were imprinted by the flash and heat at the time of the explosion.

23

be more intense or widespread than from any other groundburst, but would stay radioactive for considerably longer, requiring survivors to stay in shelters for months.

Having considered the effects of each of the separate features of the nuclear explosion we should also consider their effect when combined. Experience seems to indicate that immediate deaths are due to a single cause, i.e. blast alone or burns alone, but that death some time after the explosion may well be due to combined causes. For example, burns place considerable stress on the blood system and radiation exposure impairs the blood's ability to support recovery and fight infection. A further cause of death is the possible combination of injuries and environmental damage. After the attack people will be without services for sanitation, heating, etc. and will be living in squalid conditions in very cramped shelters.

As the US Congress Office of Technology Assessment concluded:

'Throughout all the uncertainties and qualifications included here, one theme is constant: that nuclear war would be catastrophic on a scale unprecedented in history, since its effects would last for generations.'[2] ■

Questions for Study and Discussion

A Nuclear Attack on Britain
1. Drawing on the results of the Pontifical Academy of Sciences on the effects of nuclear war, Pope John Paul II has made the statement that conditions following a nuclear attack would be so severe that the only hope for humanity is prevention of any form of nuclear war. In the light of the scenario presented in this section, do you agree with his statement? What would prevention involve?
2. Discuss Dr Sasaki's statement: 'I see that they are holding a trial for war criminals in Tokyo just now. I think they ought to try the men who decided to use the bomb and they should hang them all.'

Weapon Effects
3. What are the five ways the energy of a nuclear explosion is released?
4. Give some examples of combinations of effects of a nuclear explosion.

5. Why would the effects of a nuclear war last for generations? In your mind does this make nuclear war significantly different from conventional warfare?

Notes: Weapon Effects
1. Office of Technology Assessment, Congress of the United States, *The Effects of Nuclear War*, ch. 2, (Croom Helm, London 1980)
2. Ibid.

Nuclear Strategy

'Thus far the chief purpose of our military establishment has been to win wars. From now on its chief purpose must be to avert them. It can have no other useful purpose.'[1]

So wrote the American military strategist, Bernard Brodie, in 1945 to explain the difference that the advent of nuclear weapons had made to the usefulness of force in the postwar world. This approach to military force came to be known as 'deterrence' – the use of threats to discourage military action by other nations – and thus to prevent war.

Deterrence is still the main concept used to justify the possession of nuclear weapons and the threat to use them: we hold these weapons not to fight a war but to prevent one happening. This is a very appealing way of presenting a case for nuclear weapons. It emphasises that their existence is primarily for defensive, not aggressive purposes, that they contribute to peace, indeed that they are necessary for peace. While 'deterrence' may still be the correct term to apply to present-day nuclear strategy, its meaning has changed over the years and there are good reasons to doubt the validity of the concept. In order to show this we look at some of the changes that have taken place in thinking and planning for the use of nuclear weapons.

Mutually Assured Destruction

The 1960's saw the development of a strategic doctrine of nuclear deterrence called 'mutually assured destruction' (often shortened appropriately to MAD!). This doctrine took into account the fact that the USA and the USSR each had the ability to obliterate the other using nuclear weapons. It also embodied the best known version of deterrence: two 'rational' nations in conflict with each other are deterred from attacking one another by the threat that unacceptable damage by nuclear weapons will be inflicted on their civilian populations.

'The civilian population is chosen, despite laws of war and moral considerations to the contrary, on the grounds that an attack on it is what hurts most and so deters most effectively.'[2]

Neat calculations were done in the Pentagon (the United States Department of Defence) to determine how much damage would be 'unacceptable' to the Soviets. A figure of 20 to 30% of the population of the USSR was thought to be enough.[3] The role of nuclear missiles and bombs was to guarantee that this level of destruction could actually be carried out. They were not, according to the doctrine, seen as weapons which could be used to fight and win a war, since it was assumed that if a nuclear war were to occur the level of destruction on both sides would be so great that it would be meaningless to talk of 'winners'.[4]

From the point of view of maintaining peace the attractiveness of the MAD strategy lies in the fact that there is no incentive for either side to start a war. The fact that both sides are able to *assure* the destruction of the other even after they have themselves been attacked means that there is nothing to be gained by firing the first shot. According to this reasoning both sides are 'self-deterred', that is, they refrain from using their weapons first because of their knowledge of the likely consequences: the use of nuclear weapons appears 'unthinkable'. At a time of international tension this reluctance to shoot first would obviously be very valuable in preventing a nuclear war from starting. Strategists talk of 'stability' or 'instability' in a crisis between nations, depending on whether the circumstances put pressure on governments to exercise restraint or to make an early attack. In theory a strategy based on mutually assured destruction leads to restraint and stability.

Mutually assured destruction is still commonly regarded as being what nuclear arms are all about and it is true that both sides have a far greater ability now to assure each other's destruction than they did during the 1960's. However, since the early 1970's military planning in the USA and NATO have changed dramatically.

Deterrence of the kind described above has proved unappealing to politicians and distasteful to men in the military establishment.[5] However, for a long time the state of technological achievement would not allow anything else. Nuclear weapons were so destructive and imprecise and the systems for co-ordinating an attack so clumsy, that they could not be used in a more traditional military role. So, with reluctance, they were relegated to the status of 'ultimate deterrent' which meant that they were effectively unusable in other than 'ultimate circumstances' such as a nuclear attack on the USA or a Soviet invasion of western Europe.

Dissatisfaction with MAD in the highest quarters was made public in 1970 when President Nixon questioned the right of a president to only have 'the single option of ordering the mass destruction of enemy civilians in the face of the certainty that it would be followed by the mass slaughter of Americans'.[6] This question highlights the horror and futility of carrying out the threat to inflict 'unacceptable damage' on the enemy. It also expresses the frustration and sense of powerlessness of the man in command of the world's most destructive military force. To put it in colourful language, he can do nothing with his weaponry until the worst is upon him and then he is supposed to mindlessly unleash the lot in a blind, futile and suicidal gesture! To make matters even worse, the fact that this would be such an extreme, irrational and self-destructive act might well make it seem unlikely that he would ever choose to carry it out. In other words, the threat is so crazy that the enemy might not believe it and a threat that is not believed is an ineffective one as far as influencing the enemy is concerned.

Implicitly President Nixon was asking that greater flexibility be introduced into the plans for the use of nuclear weapons. He wanted choices to be open to him which were more limited in nature and which could be used to achieve a particular 'flexible' approach. We will call this doctrine 'flexible response'. (It is also called 'limited stra-

1 Thurso
2 Kinloss
3 Edzell
4 Leuchars
5 Rosyth
6 Grangemouth
7 Edinburgh
8 Glasgow
9 Holy Loch
10 Faslane
11 Hunterston
12 Glasgow airport
13 Macrihanish
14 Omagh
15 Belfast
16 Boulmer
17 Newcastle airport
18 Newcastle
19 Fylingdales
20 Teesport
21 North Tees
22 Calder Hall
23 Windscale
24 Catterick
25 Topcliffe
26 Harrogate
27 Bradford
28 Leeds
29 Killingholme
30 Hull
31 Immingham
32 Grimsby
33 Binbrook
34 Coningsby
35 Digby
36 Waddington
37 Cranwell
38 Scampton
39 Nottingham
40 Castle Donington
41 Derby
42 Sheffield
43 Manchester
44 Stanlow/Ellesmere Port
45 Liverpool
46 Valley
47 Northwood
48 Criggion
49 Sculthorpe
50 Coltishall
51 West Raynham
52 Honington
53 Marham

◆ oil refinery
⊙ Royal Air Force
☆ US Air Force
△ submarine base
● industrial target
□ other military targets

BRITAIN'S NUCLEAR TARGETS

26

tegic options', or 'the Schlesinger doctrine' after the then Secretary of Defence, James Schlesinger.)

The New Doctrine

Flexible response is an attempt to get away from some of the inadequacies of 'pure' deterrence and to make nuclear weapons useful as instruments of war. The idea that nuclear war must always be total war is refuted and with it the notion that any use of nuclear weapons is unthinkable. This paves the way for the threat to use these weapons in less extreme circumstances, and (it is hoped) makes the threat believable. The impact of this on deterrence is to break down the distinction between nuclear and conventional weapons. The force of nuclear threats no longer lies in the capacity to destroy the enemy's society but in the ability to fight and win a war. Nuclear weapons, like conventional weapons, become capable not only of defence but of offence and coercion as soon as their use is separated from total war. In reality it has not proved possible to guarantee that a small scale nuclear exchange would not lead quickly to world war, destroying both East and West. This is a restraint and makes the use of the term 'deterrence' still somewhat applicable. However, the determination is there to free nuclear weapons from the restriction that their limited use is unthinkable. In practical terms flexible response means two things. Firstly, there is an emphasis on being able to attack *military* targets with nuclear weapons. This is called 'counterforce', since it is the enemy's forces and not his cities that are targeted. Secondly, rather than making one particular threat to destroy enemy society, a very wide range of *limited* uses of nuclear weapons is available. These can be combined and tailored with flexibility to match any circumstances. Each of these aspects has important implications.

Counterforce

There has long been a school of strategists in the USA which has promoted the idea of counterforce as opposed to counter-city targeting. The picture that this school paints of a likely nuclear war emphasises the need to develop the ability to deliver a crushing blow to the enemy's forces, particularly his nuclear forces. This view of nuclear war has important implications for peace. It can be said to weaken the

incentive to avoid starting a war. In some circumstances it may actually lead one or other side to the conclusion that it must strike first to avoid being destroyed.

To understand this, compare counterforce with the MAD approach. MAD is basically a hostage strategy in which the cities and population of the enemy country are held as hostages who will be destroyed if the opponent attacks. The security for each side lies in knowing that the enemy believes this threat. This makes it of the utmost importance for the nuclear forces to be safe from an attack so that they will be able to deliver a retaliatory blow – a 'second strike'. (Submarine-launched missiles are an example of an invulnerable weapon system since a submarine can hide in the depths of the ocean.) If both sides have adequate invulnerable weapons then stability is improved in two ways. Firstly, neither side wishes to strike first since it knows it cannot destroy the enemy's ability to retaliate and so risks being destroyed itself. Secondly, both sides know there is no need to panic. They have weapons which are protected and will survive a nuclear attack. They each know that the other side also knows these weapons will survive. So both sides know that the opponent cannot hope to gain anything from attacking first. This means that there is no pressure to 'get your blow in before he does' or, in the language of strategists, to attack pre-emptively.

This situation is radically changed with the advent of flexible response as the US and NATO's strategic doctrine. The important thing is to be able to destroy the enemy's ability to retaliate. We are not yet in a situation where either side has this capability – for one thing submarines remain relatively invulnerable. But steady improvements in technology have made the land-based intercontinental missiles on both sides increasingly vulnerable to a surprise attack and it is likely that Soviet submarine-launched missile forces will also soon be at risk.[7]

The dangers of this situation are obvious. If one or both sides believe that they can destroy the enemy's retaliatory capability – that is, they believe they can *win* a war by striking first without risk of retaliation – then they cease to be self-deterred. The arguments which show that MAD leads to stability are turned on their heads. The fear of being destroyed in retaliation or revenge is removed or greatly lessened. The fear that the enemy may strike first becomes very real because he can destroy the possibility of retaliation. In a crisis this could conceivably put pressure on one side, through fear, to make a pre-emptive first strike – to get its blow in first.

One much publicised way in which deterrence can be retained in this situation is to threaten that missiles will be launched in the few minutes between the detection by satellite of an enemy attack and the missiles arriving at their targets. (This was hinted at by US Secretary of State, Cyrus Vance, in a television discussion in 1979.) This would put doubt in the mind of the enemy that his attack would succeed in destroying the opponent's nuclear forces or that he would escape with only acceptable damage. However, such an approach puts forces of immense destructive capability on a very fine trigger indeed. In fact, Pershing II (see p. 34) will only take eight minutes from the time it is launched in West Germany to reach its target in Russia. Because of this, the only possible response can be by computer.

Limited Nuclear War

The flexible response doctrine brought with it an emphasis on limiting and controlling the progress of a nuclear war. Unlimited nuclear war would incinerate all the participant nations. Such an enormous and suicidal threat may well be credible as a response to an all-out Soviet attack but it might lack credibility in less extreme circumstances. If the USSR chose to gain large objectives in a series of small steps, each one carefully calculated to be too insignificant to justify an all-out nuclear war the west would be impotent to act. However, if a war could be limited, and the scope of the conflict kept within certain boundaries, then the use of nuclear weapons could be convincingly threatened in response to lesser Soviet actions.

The development of counterforce technology, which includes improved systems for command and control of forces and the miniaturisation of warheads, has led to the widespread belief in the US government and military that nuclear war can be limited. Secretary of Defence, James Schlesinger, affirmed this belief when he introduced the flexible response doctrine in 1974.[8]

The capacity to make 'limited' nuclear strikes means one also has the capacity to withhold higher levels of force which remain to threaten the opponent even once nuclear war has started. The threat can be used as a deterrent within the war to prevent the enemy from going any further. In Europe, for example, flexible response means meeting any aggression at the level at which it is made. So an attack with conventional weapons will be met by a similar defence. If NATO starts to lose, it will use nuclear weapons, before the Warsaw Pact* does, if necessary. The nuclear attack will be made at a particular limited level of violence, giving the Warsaw Pact the choice of giving up, of retaliating in kind, or of responding even more violently. However, the restraint of the first NATO attack implies the threat of a higher level of violence which has not yet been used (perhaps against a Warsaw Pact city if the earlier attack was on military forces). The highest level of violence would then be reserved for use against the population of the USSR. This threat would deter the enemy from going any further and ensure that there was an incentive for giving up – that is the survival of his cities. This sort of deterrence (called 'intra-war deterrence'), relying on limited, flexible targeting, is seen as a way of keeping nuclear war within limits.

The possibility of control is of course an assumption which has never been tested and there are two strong reasons for doubting its validity. The first is to do with the nature of nuclear war itself. Many strategists believe that once hostilities break out the chance of controlling one's own weapons is slim. Systems which operate in peacetime for communication, command and control may rapidly break down in the extreme conditions of a nuclear war and military personnel may act in unpredictable ways. NATO 'war games', simulating nuclear war, have apparently on several occasions led to obliteration of both sides.

A second factor which makes the hope of limiting a nuclear war seem optimistic is the attitude of the opponent. The USSR has not given any indication that it accepts the rules of the limited nuclear war game. On the contrary Soviet military writings continue to assert that in the event of nuclear war its forces, far from exercising moderation and restraint, will strike simultaneously at all significant targets.[9] This quite naturally worries US strategists, but they hope that as on some other issues the Soviet Union might

be brought round to seeing things their way as Soviet technology improves.[10]

Even if both of these problems were to be resolved, the control of war would rely on a calm and rational approach on both sides. They would have to stop when the 'costs' of continuing started to outweigh the 'benefits'. They would have to be able to make such calculations, and at each stage they would need to be aware of the level of violence directed against them and the intentions which lay behind it. Otherwise they would overreact and things would be likely to get out of hand. Doubts about the reliability and accuracy of weapons are likely in desperate circumstances to lead to the traditional military remedy – saturation bombing.[11] Despite these doubts, the concept of limited nuclear war as a cornerstone of flexible response remains an essential part of present-day strategy. Measures are taken, as far as possible, to eliminate the sources of doubt. For example, vulnerable command and communication facilities have been protected and hardened against attack, and smaller more 'discriminating' nuclear weapons, such as the neutron bomb, have been developed. We must hope that the US and NATO leadership never come to the point of believing that they have succeeded in limiting nuclear war. For, while the ability to make credible threats is presented as a strengthening of deterrence, it would simultaneously remove the most significant restraint on the use of nuclear weapons: the fear that war would get horribly out of control.

Finally, the use of the word 'limited' might be misleading. A study by the US Defence Department in 1975 concluded the following: A Soviet strike against the US strategic missile force alone would cause 5.6 million deaths, and destroy 42% of the silos*. A heavier strike would cause 18.3 million deaths, and destroy 80% of the silos.[12] This was confirmed by a report of the US Congress Office of Technology Assessment, published in 1980 which estimated that, depending on conditions, up to 20 million people might die in a Soviet attack restricted to US missile and bomber bases. A similar American attack on the USSR might claim the lives of more than 10 million of the more dispersed Soviet population.[13] Focusing on Europe, the massive German study by Carl Friedrick von Weizsäcker concluded that:

* see glossary, p.116

'Even a brief and locally limited war could mean ten million deaths and cause total destruction of West Germany as an industrial society. Escalation to blind utilization of existing weapons' capabilities could mean the extinction of all life in Germany. Von Weizsäcker is reported as having testified elsewhere, in studies for the NATO Nuclear Planning Group, that an input of just 10 per cent of the nuclear weapons now stationed in Europe could practically annihilate both East and West Germany.'[14]

These are all estimates of the likely effects of a war which would be called 'limited', either by a choice of targets which did not include cities or by a geographical limitation to the continent of Europe. If, as seems likely, the war were to escalate uncontrollably the casualty figures would be unimaginable. The same 1980 report referred to above concludes that in a war involving very large attacks against a range of military and economic targets, deaths in the USA would range

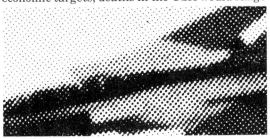

from 70 to 160 million and in the USSR from 50 to 100 million. If populations were deliberately targeted an additional 20 to 30 million people would die on each side. These statistics however 'reflect only deaths during the first thirty days. Additional millions would be injured, and many would eventually die from lack of adequate medical care. In addition millions of people might starve or freeze during the following winter but it is not possible to estimate how many.'[15] Further millions might eventually die of long-term radiation effects.

The move towards counterforce is a move to increased instability and the risk that, in a crisis, war could be sparked off through fear. The teaching that war could be limited would also reduce inhibitions against the use of nuclear weapons. The optimism of the strategist may turn out to be unfounded with all-out war ensuing. But even within conditions of control and limitation the destruction would be so immense that it is hard to see how flexible response can be described as a defence.

* see glossary, p.116

Questions for Study and Discussion
Nuclear Strategy

1. How does the strategy of 'mutually assured destruction' limit the incentive to start a war? What are the shortcomings of this strategy (from a military point of view) that have resulted in the move to 'flexible response'?
2. What are the differences between 'mutually assured destruction' and 'counterforce' strategy? How does 'counterforce' strategy affect deterrence?
3. Why does the ability to 'limit' a nuclear war make it seem more believable? Do you find it convincing that nuclear war could be limited?

Notes: Nuclear Strategy

1. Bernard Brodie quoted in Daniel Yergin, *Shattered Peace* (Penguin, 1980), 478.
2. Robert Neild, *How To Make Up Your Mind About The Bomb* (André Deutsch, 1981), 49.
3. A. C. Enthoven, '1963 Nuclear Strategy Revisited', in *Ethics and Nuclear Strategy,* ed. H. P. Ford and F. X. Winters (Orbis, 1977), 76.
4. Ibid., 76-77.
5. *World Armaments and Disarmament, SIPRI Yearbook 1981* (Taylor and Francis, 1981), ch 2.
6. Dan Smith, *The Defence of the Realm in the 1980's* (Croom Helm, 1980), 44.
7. J. S. Wit, 'Advances in Antisubmarine Warfare', *Scientific American,* 244, no. 2 (Feb. 1981).
   F. Barnaby, 'Death beneath the Waves', *New Scientist,* 27 Sept. 1979.
8. *World Armaments and Disarmament, SIPRI Yearbook 1975* (Almquist and Wiksell, Stockholm 1975), 44.
9. B. Lambeth, 'Selective Nuclear Operations and Soviet Strategy' in *Beyond Nuclear Disarmament: New Aims, New Arms* (Crane, Russak and Co., 1977) 87.
10. H. S. Rowen and A. Wohlstetter, 'Varying Response with Circumstances', in *Beyond Nuclear Disarmament: New Aims, New Arms* (Crane, Russak and Co., 1977), 226-227.
11. *SIPRI Yearbook 1981,* 43.
12. Quoted in *Scientific American,* (Nov. 1976).
13. Office of Technology Assessment, Congress of the United States, *The Effects of Nuclear War* (Croom Helm, 1980), 7.
14. Alva Myrdal, *The Game of Disarmament* (Spokesman, 1980), 42.
15. Office of Technology Assessment, *The Effects of Nuclear War,* 8.

Britain and Nuclear Weapons

The United Kingdom was in at the very start of the nuclear era. She participated during World War II with the USA and Canada in the successful Manhattan Project which culminated in the first test of a nuclear weapon at Alamogordo in New Mexico on 16 July 1945. The Quebec Agreement of August 1943 said, among other things, that none of the three powers would use an atomic bomb without the consent of the others. The decision to drop bombs on Hiroshima and Nagasaki on 6 and 9 August 1945 was essentially an American one, but the consent of the British Government was asked for and given by Winston Churchill.[1] Although by the end of the war Britain was clearly a junior partner in nuclear affairs, she had come to see herself as rightfully a nuclear power.

At the end of the war the USA was reluctant to continue the co-operation over nuclear matters and the British Government decided to develop its own programme. The first British atom bomb was tested in 1952 and the first hydrogen bomb some four years later. Since that time the United Kingdom has acquired a wide range of nuclear weapons and systems for delivering them to their targets. Every British Government since that war has continued the policy of maintaining a British nuclear force.

The Situation Today

Britain has its own substantial nuclear weapons research and development programme at the Atomic Weapons Research Establishment at Aldermaston near Reading. Five thousand people are employed there at a cost of £100 million a year. Aldermaston shares in the production of nuclear weapons along with two Royal Ordnance Factories at Burghfield and Cardiff. In addition to weapons designed and produced in the UK, Britain owns, or can use, a number of nuclear weapons which are wholly or partly produced in the USA. Others are produced jointly with other NATO countries.

British Strategic Nuclear Weapons

1. *Polaris*

Britain has four submarines which each carry 16 Polaris A3 missiles. These are based at Faslane on the lower Clyde. Every 3½ years the submarines have to undergo a re-fit lasting about 18 months. These are carried out at Rosyth on the river Forth. The length and frequency of these overhauls mean that never more than two submarines, and often only one, are on patrol at any one time. Each Polaris missile carries a warhead which divides into three 200 kiloton 're-entry vehicles', all of which travel to the same target. A new warhead named 'Chevaline', has been developed at Aldermaston for the Polaris missile. It is designed to improve the ability to penetrate anti-missile defences such as those around Moscow. Chevaline is able to manoeuvre in space although the re-entry vehicles are not targeted independently. It may carry up to six warheads or a combination of warheads and decoys.

2. *Trident*

The Trident II system, which was ordered from the USA by the British Government early in 1982, is intended to replace the ageing Polaris system in the 1990's. Four new submarines will be built, each of which will carry 16 Trident D5 missiles. The warhead for the missile will be MIRVed* and may carry 14 re-entry vehicles. Since each re-entry vehicle can be independently targeted the number of targets which can be attacked will be fourteen times greater than with Polaris. A single Trident submarine could theoretically destroy 224 targets. This is much more than enough to threaten every large city in the USSR. Trident will also be considerably more accurate than Polaris and will almost certainly be capable of destroying Soviet missiles in their

* see glossary, p.116

silos. It is thus a formidable counterforce weapon whereas Polaris is only accurate enough to destroy cities.

The decision to buy the Trident system, while alarming and abhorrent to opponents of nuclear weapons, has been controversial even in circles which favour reliance on nuclear weapons. The controversy centres partly around the need for this kind of weapon and partly around the cost involved.

The purchase of Trident represents an enormous increase in destructive power. It also signifies a shift towards counterforce and therefore a warfighting capability. It is extremely difficult to imagine the possible value of such a system to the United Kingdom. If Polaris has been regarded as an adequate deterrent throughout the 1970's the question is raised: What has changed that requires this new capability? Dan Smith, reviewing the arguments for Britain's independent nuclear force, concludes that basically irrational motives are involved: it is important for Britain's sense of her own significance that she have a prestigious advanced missile system however irrelevant to her needs.[2]

The sophistication of Trident makes its purchase not only an expensive and useless indulgence but a dangerous one. The US government has deliberately developed the Trident II missile as a counter-force, war-fighting weapon.[2A] Great missile accuracy is combined with the capacity of a submarine to attack from close to the target and from any angle. This would give the opponent very little time before his own missiles were destroyed. Trident II is thus a great threat to the Russian capacity to retaliate since the bulk of Soviet nuclear forces are land-based missiles. Faced with this threat of an extremely rapid first strike it would not be surprising if the USSR firmly adopted a 'launch-on-warning' policy. This would be an extremely dangerous situation.

In acquiring Trident the United Kingdom is participating in (and partly funding) this dangerous development. It is also clearly re-arming unilaterally, increasing both the number of missiles and their effectiveness. This is provocative and seems likely to feed the already intensifying atmosphere of hostility between East and West.

The cost of procuring the Trident II System was given at £7,500 million at September 1981 prices. This will be spread over 15 years at about £500 million per year. The announcement came during a period of cuts in the expenditure on conventional forces, especially those of the Royal Navy, and it is apparent that money will have to be found for Trident from expenditure which would otherwise go to conventional forces. The fact that this choice would have to be made was foreseeable, and indeed was foreseen. Writing before the Trident decision was announced Lawrence Freedman says of the Government's decision to increase defence expenditure by 3% annually in line with NATO policy:

'The problem is quite straightforward: 3 per cent is sufficient to maintain the existing defence effort but not to branch out into new types of activity. This is because of the high relative cost of each succeeding generation of military equipment, as well as the need to maintain highly skilled volunteer forces with competitive wages and salaries. The 3 per cent is needed to stand still.'[3]

In a similar vein, Dan Smith writes of the unresolved dilemma between 'available resources' (money) and 'desired capabilities'. He argues that the desire for an impressive military posture has led to an insufficient expenditure on back up resources and pay.

'It is all very well keeping a rounded force posture with sophisticated weapon systems at its core, but not a great deal of it makes sense when RAF transport is cut right back, fuel and spare parts are in short supply, forces' living conditions inadequate, recruitment low and early departure from the forces high.'[4]

Using an unofficial estimate of the cost of replacing Polaris he concludes:

'This would absorb a large proportion of the equipment budget throughout the 1980's, making one wonder what other weapons projects the armed forces would be willing to sacrifice.'[5]

The choice between this new nuclear force and adequate conventional defence is therefore a real and controversial one. The criticism is even more severe from those who would have the £7.5 billion spent on hospitals, schools or overseas aid.

3. Tornado

One other significant weapon is the Tornado aircraft. The Tornado is being produced jointly by Britain, West Germany and Italy. Britain will be taking 385 planes of which 220 will be nuclear

HMS Resolution, Britain's first nuclear submarine commissioned on October 2nd, 1967, armed with 16 Polaris missiles capable of being delivered with extreme accuracy at a range of 2,500 nautical miles.

capable. This aircraft would be able to carry a nuclear-tipped air-launched cruise missile (possibly a variant of the Sea Eagle missile being developed by British Aerospace). Its range of around 800 miles would allow it to reach the western-most part of the Soviet Union. If Trident were to be cancelled, Tornado might well become the basis for a continued British strategic nuclear deterrent.

Tactical and Theatre Nuclear Weapons

In addition to the 'strategic' nuclear force, Britain has a nuclear capability at the theatre and tactical level. It should be noted that at this level also there is an increase in nuclear capability in all three branches of the armed services. Thus, for example, the British Army is more than doubling the number of artillery pieces which can deliver nuclear shells; the RAF is increasing from more than 200 to over 300 its nuclear capable aircraft and the Royal Navy is increasing its force of nuclear capable helicopters as well as adding the Sea Harrier which is nuclear capable.[6]

Another fact which may be even more important is that nuclear weapons are integrated into the weaponry of the forces.[7] The aircraft, ships and artillery which carry out conventional non-nuclear missions are the same as those which carry and deliver nuclear weapons. As a result it seems likely that a conventional war with the Soviet Union would quickly escalate to the nuclear level.

In addition to United Kingdom nuclear weapons it must be remembered that Britain is used as a base for American nuclear weapons. These include the fleet of Poseidon Submarines and the F1 11 aircraft. A decision has been taken by NATO to base a number of American Cruise missiles in Britain. This addition will have important consequences and is worth considering in some detail.

The Cruise Missile

On 12 December 1979 NATO decided on a programme of 'modernisation' of the nuclear forces in the European Theatre.* The plan involved the deployment of 572 additional nuclear missiles in 5 European countries. Of these, 108 would be Pershing II missiles sited in West Germany and 464 would be cruise missiles – 160 of which are to be sited in the United Kingdom. It is planned that 96 of the cruise missiles will be based at Greenham Common in Berkshire by the end of 1983, and a further 64 at Molesworth in Cambridgeshire in 1988. The missiles will be entirely under American control.

Cruise missiles are small pilotless aircraft which fly at low altitudes to avoid radar detection. They fly at the subsonic speed of 500 m.p.h. The navigation system for cruise missiles is extremely sophisticated; called 'terrain contour matching' it involves surveying the terrain with radar and comparing the readings with a map which is stored on a computer. This system, it is claimed, allows the missile to follow an indirect route to the target which it can then strike with very great accuracy. The Pershing II is a highly accurate intermediate range ballistic missile,*

This page: RAF Nimrod, high altitude surveillance plane (Opposite): USA Navy Polaris missile on test launch.

capable of reaching Moscow from West Germany.

The reason given for the introduction of these new missiles is that they will redress an imbalance which it is claimed exists in the nuclear forces in the European Theatre. A great deal of publicity has been given to this supposed imbalance, emphasising the new mobile Soviet SS20 missiles which are highly accurate, and carry three independently targeted warheads. In fact the decision appears to owe as much to the internal politics of NATO as to any external threat.[8]

The decision by the British Government to support the plans for 'modernisation' and especially to accept cruise missiles onto British soil is a highly controversial one. Jeff McMahan, in his book *British Nuclear Weapons*, examines the case for cruise missiles and comes to the following conclusions.

1. *Cruise missiles will not improve deterrence*

One of the main arguments for introducing cruise missiles is that they present a more 'credible' threat to the USSR than do the strategic missiles* based in the United States. The risk of Soviet retaliation might be thought to deter the use of American strategic missiles in the event of a Soviet attack on Western Europe. McMahan believes that basing the missiles in Europe will make no difference in this way. As American weapons under exclusive control of the US their use would most likely bring Soviet retaliation directly against the US homeland. The inhibitions on their use would therefore be just as great as those on the use of American ICBMs.** As land-based missiles they are vulnerable to a Soviet first-strike attack: either a surprise attack on their bases or, if the missiles have been dispersed, air burst saturation attacks with very large bombs over the areas where the missiles are suspected of being ... a rather sobering reflection for people living in the South East of England and the Midlands![9]

2. *Cruise missiles are potentially destabilising*

In a time of international crisis cruise missiles make nuclear war more likely. The fact that they are accurate enough to destroy hardened military targets means that the Russians could not afford to 'ride out' an attack in which they would fear losing their missiles. The slowness in flight of the

* see glossary, p.116

** (ICBM) see Appendix, p.117

cruise missile would allow the Russians the time to launch their own missiles on warning that an attack had been launched. An 'accidental firing of a cruise missile or misinterpretation of radar data – and the latter is particularly likely, given the difficulty of detecting cruise missiles – could trigger a massive retaliatory strike and thus lead to nuclear war.'[10]

3. *Cruise missiles are provocative*

As counterforce weapons with a degree of accuracy which is only necessary if they are to be used to strike first, cruise missiles must look to the USSR like *offensive* rather than *defensive* weapons. Therefore they greatly increase the level of threat to the Soviet Union in a way that is reminiscent of the threat experienced by the USA when Russian missiles were going to be placed in Cuba in 1962.

'The cruise missiles will be liberally spread around close to Russia's borders; they will be capable of striking almost 500 miles deeper into Russian territory than the US FIIIs; and they will be wholly under American control.'[11]

McMahan concludes, 'In short, the case for rejecting the American cruise missiles is overwhelming.'

Conclusions

The question of British nuclear defence policy is presented in its most urgent form by Cruise and Trident. These weapons represent imminent and disturbing changes in the status-quo in both the quantity and the nature of British-based nuclear forces. It is for this reason that we have devoted most of this section to a consideration of these two weapon systems.

The wider question still remains, of course, as to whether Britain should renounce nuclear weapons altogether as a basis for defence. The case for this on moral grounds is developed in Part II. A strong case can also be made on the basis of Britain's actual defence requirements, arguing that Britain's own nuclear force brings no observable benefit; that, along with American nuclear bases, they reduce security by making this island one of the highest priority targets for nuclear attack; and that British nuclear disarmament could pave the way for more general multilateral disarmament which is at an impasse. A full discussion of these arguments for and against Britain's nuclear disarmament is beyond the scope of this study, but is developed in some detail in Robert Neild, *How To Make Up Your Mind About The Bomb*.[12]

Questions for Study and Discussion

Britain and Nuclear Weapons

1. Since there is an unresolved dilemma between 'available resources' (money) and 'desired capabilities' choices must be made between maintaining 'adequate' conventional forces and updating the nuclear force. Which do you think is a higher priority?

2. What are the main differences between Polaris and Trident II submarine launched missiles? Do you feel the introduction of Trident is necessary?

3. How would cruise missiles affect the relationship between Russia and the USA in a crisis? Imagine yourself as a Soviet leader – how would you view the deployment of these weapons?

Notes: Britain and Nuclear Weapons

1. Winston Churchill, *The Second World War* (Cassell), VI, 553.
2. Dan Smith, 'After Polaris', in K. Coates, ed., *Eleventh Hour for Europe* (Spokesman, 1981).
2A. Joel S. Wit, 'American SLBM: Counterforce Options and Strategic Implications', in *Survival* 24 (4) 1982.
3. Lawrence Freedman, *Britain and Nuclear Weapons* (Macmillan, 1980), 84.
4. Dan Smith, *The Defence of the Realm in the 1980's* (Croom Helm, 1980), 121.
5. Ibid., 127.
6. Rogers, P.; Dando, M.; van den Dungen, P., *As Lambs to the Slaughter* (London, Arrow, 1981), 58-64.
7. Rogers et. al. Op. cit. 64, 98-100.
8. Lawrence Freedman, *Britain and Nuclear Weapons,* 117 ff.
   US Library of Congress Research Service, 'The Evolution of NATO's Decision to "Modernise" Theatre Nuclear Weapons', in Alva Myrdal and others, *Dynamics of European Nuclear Disarmament* (Spokesman, 1981).
9. Phil Bolsover, *Civil Defence: The Cruellest Confidence Trick* (CND, 1980).
10. Alexander R. Vershbow, 'The Cruise Missile, The End of Arms Control?', *Foreign Affairs*, 55, no. 1 (Oct. 1976), 110, 111.
11. Jeff McMahan, *British Nuclear Weapons, For and Against* (Junction Books, 1981), 111.
12. Robert Neild, *How To Make Up Your Mind About The Bomb* (André Deutsch, 1981).

Civil Defence

One of the most important aspects of preparation for fighting a nuclear war is civil defence. Unwilling to meet the enormous cost of providing shelters for the population, the Government has been running a vigorous publicity campaign to encourage 'do-it-yourself' civil defence measures. For those who cannot afford the cost of their own underground shelter (they cost anything from a few hundred pounds to over £12,000), the Government's pamphlet 'Protect and Survive' purports to provide guidance on 'sensible' measures to take in the event of a nuclear attack and in preparation for one. This pamphlet, when it was released in May 1980, provoked widespread alarm, both because it made nuclear war seem more likely and, because its instruction that each household should prepare a 'refuge room', brought the possibility of war right into each home. The Government, aware that it had aroused fear and opposition, modified its civil defence policy in the Autumn of 1980. Instead of emphasising the need for refuge rooms, table shelters and white-washed windows, it started to concentrate on involving local organisations: Parish Councils, Women's Institutes, the WRVS etc. An 'only you can save yourselves' approach was adopted. This policy, linking voluntary groups and local government, has the advantage of winning support for civil defence planning by involving ordinary people at a grass-roots level.

The instruction in 'Protect and Survive' to stay at home in the event of a nuclear attack is a change from the 1960's policy of evacuation for women and children. It is intended to prevent public disorder but in certain areas would ensure the incineration of vast numbers of people. A glance at 'Operation Square Leg' for example (a Home Defence exercise simulating a nuclear attack on Britain) shows that for anyone living in Glasgow or a major city the safest place to be would *not* be at home! With this fact comes the unpleasant realisation that civil defence is not primarily about saving life but about preparing for war. In the House of Commons debate (21 February 1980) Mr. Leon Brittan, Minister of State, Home Office, mentioned one reason for the campaign. It was essential, he said, that

'civil preparedness should be adequate if the credibility of the military deterrent strategy was to be maintained. Military and civil preparedness was closely related.'[1]

Civil defence plans are a psychological preparation for war. As Phil Bolsover states in 'Civil Defence: the Cruellest Confidence Trick':

'The Government must indeed hope that its Home Defence plans will enable some people to survive. That is praiseworthy enough ... But it also hopes to accustom us to the idea of nuclear war; to persuade us that individually we will live even though others die ... The manufacture of this atmosphere is as much a preparation for war, as is manufacture of a hydrogen bomb.'

In stark contrast to the minimal preparations for the protection of the population are those for the Government and military personnel. As hostilities draw near the national Government will go underground in its protected deep bunker, at West Wells Road, Hawthorn, near Corsham, in Wiltshire, capable of holding 25-50,000 people. Scotland would be governed from a giant concrete bunker next to the A71 at Kirknewton. The ten armed forces' headquarters in England and Wales, the three zone headquarters in Scotland and the numerous sub-regional headquarters are similarly protected. As E. P. Thompson has pointed out in his booklet 'Protest and Survive', the British Government is busily preparing for nuclear war, its political leaders planning

'to survive in deep, costly shelters while letting ordinary people, who thought the government's job was to protect its people, burn to death or

perish under the rubble of their devastated homes.'[2]

The Home Office Civil Defence organisation is shaped like a pyramid with the Regional Government Headquarters at the top. The organisation passes down through various sub-regions, County and District Councils, to Parish Councils and Wards of Neighbourhood groups. Here at grass-roots levels it is planned that vigilante groups will be established to safeguard against gangs of bullies, to protect food and clothing stocks and to restrain and punish dissenters.

Behind the Government's plans for the time before and after a nuclear attack there is a pre-occupation with the total regimentation of the population; an underlying fear of the people. The plans of the Civil Defence authorities depend on the willing obedience of the population. But what if a bitter, disillusioned and angry population refuses to be governed? Must they be forced to co-operate? After an attack, the Government, from its bunkers, the regional and sub-regional commissioners, and the local controllers, backed by police and soldiers would be attempting to direct us. Various means have been devised to guard against dissent. In the Police Manual of Home Defence (1974) there is a section on the additional tasks for police in a war emergency. The manual talks of

'special measures to maintain internal security, with particular reference to the detention or restriction of movement of subversive, or potentially subversive people.'

In addition to the arrest of potential subversives, police are to control crowds fleeing from cities and possible target areas in the country. Most major roads would be designated essential service routes and would be available for official traffic only. One wonders what would happen when armed soldiers and police meet fleeing crowds who have been instructed by the Government to stay at home and die quietly? The Police Manual continues with directions for coping after the attack. In a section on control of the public it says:

'Principles guiding all planning for the homeless are that they should be collected into groups only for the shortest possible period and that every effort should be made to avoid large groups. These principles are dictated by the need to lessen

the danger of epidemics, to keep up morale, and to avoid the ingredients of law and order problems.'

Civil defence plans depend upon the willing obedience of the population. Yet, in the conditions following a nuclear attack, such obedience would be highly unlikely. As a result, civil defence is more about control of the population than about protecting people from the effects of a nuclear war. A Home Office circular to local authorities puts the first aim of home defence as 'to secure the UK against any internal threat'.[3] The West Sussex Survival Guide, their county war book, bears this out in its section on 'local peacekeeping'. It stresses the need to form security groups within local communities to maintain order within the law, so the Government can administer effectively. It points out that control, once lost, would be difficult to restore.

'... punishments would probably be corporal and immediate. Any form of detention may not be possible. Firm action in the early stages may prevent a deteriorating situation from getting out of hand.'

The Survival Guide then advises that the armed services should be responsible for the execution of sentences; it is undesirable that the police should be responsible.

Most civil defence exercise time is spent on the pre-attack phase. The emphasis is on maintaining law and order more than on providing food or medical supplies, about which little could be done. Initially the country would be run by the military authorities. Civilian regional governments would only be established after it becomes safe to emerge from the bunkers, anything from several weeks to three months after an attack. In 1972 reforms were passed which gave the military establishment a greater role in civil defence.

'Civilian positions were reduced or downgraded ... County councils and other local controllers may make requests of the military but they must "remain under the command of their own officers or NCOs" and may only "support the work" of local authorities if it does not prejudice their prime role ... the maintenance of law and order.'[4]

Side by side with the civilian system will be the headquarters of the armed forces, next door to the ten regional government headquarters. The mili-

tary headquarters will be staffed by senior army and police officers.

'Under new orders issued by the Home Office, local councils must nominate a single wartime controller for official approval, normally their chief executive or clerk. In appropriate circumstances, the Controller would have the power of life and death. The country, in an emergency, will be run by a clutch of Major Generals and a large bevy of district officials.'[5]

A Home Office document entitled 'Briefing Material for Wartime Controllers', 1976, states:

'In conditions in which death, destruction and injury were commonplace, such penalties as probation, fines or sentences of imprisonment would no longer be effective in dealing with the anti-social offenders.'

Communal labour and restricted rations are recommended for minor offences.

'In cases of flagrantly anti-social behaviour there might be a need for harsher penalties than would generally be acceptable in peace time. Provision for appropriate penalties not normally available to courts would be made under emergency regulations.'

What price the democracy we have paid so dearly to defend? A Home Office circular issued in January 1979 deals with the question of food in the event of nuclear war. It says:

'After nuclear attack food would be scarce, lacking in variety and unevenly distributed throughout the country. It would be prudent to plan on the assumption that no significant food imports would be received for some time, that peace time systems of food processing and distribution would cease to function ... no arrangements could ensure that every surviving household would have, say, fourteen days supply of food after attack.'

The implication that some people would starve is clear in the remark:

'Nevertheless even without food many would survive for quite long periods provided they were not too long without water.'

But the water supply would be contaminated by radio-activity and disease. The document concludes with a threat to those who do not follow official instructions.

'Any use of nuclear weapons will escalate into a general war. There is no defence against such weapons and nuclear war will destroy civilisation and perhaps exterminate mankind. To hope for salvation from civil defence is a dangerous self-deluding pipe-dream.'

Lord Zuckerman
(Chief Scientific Adviser
to Government 1964-71)

Hiding under the stairs may sound ridiculous but it could give protection against radiation if the house remained standing.

'There would be no question of implementing emergency feeding arrangements during the pre-attack for those persons who chose to ignore the government's advice to stay in their own homes.'

The authorities are instructed to take action against rioters (hungry crowds who might help themselves from ruined supermarkets?).

Civil defence? It is a psychological preparation for war, it is about the control of the population, not its protection, about how best to maintain law and order in the devastating aftermath of nuclear war. In this country civil defence preparations may also provoke a potential enemy. In Switzerland, a non-nuclear power, shelters have been built clearly as a protection against the hazards of radiation. These pose no threat to the USSR. We are a nuclear power and our civil defence preparations are quite explicitly to show that we are preparing to fight a nuclear war. To quote from Jeff McMahan's book *British Nuclear Weapons, For and Against*:

'One very important reason why civil defence preparations are undesirable in a nuclear-armed state is that they may be misunderstood by a potential enemy as a preparation for war. If a country intended to launch a first strike, one thing it would do would be to engage in civil defence preparations in order to enable it to survive any retaliation that might come.'[6]

Many councils are not participating in preparations for civil defence. One hundred and twenty-five local authorities, city councils, county councils, district councils and others have declared themselves Nuclear Free Zones. They will oppose the siting or manufacture of nuclear weapons within their boundaries and many refuse to co-operate with the Government's plans. This has had a major effect on 'Operation Hard Rock' – the next civil defence exercise, which was scheduled to have taken place in the Autumn of 1982.

Doctors from Russia and the West met in 1981 at a conference in Washington to form International Physicians for the Prevention of Nuclear War. They endorsed the statement that:

'It is an illusion that civil defence could save significant numbers of lives or significantly decrease the effects of nuclear war.'

All evidence supports Phil Bolsover's conclusion:

'You cannot save yourself on nuclear doomsday by sitting in a fallout refuge. You are your own civil defence. Your defence is action against the policy that makes you a target.'[7]

Notes: Civil Defence

1. *Times*, 22 February 1980.
2. Jim Forest and Peter Herby, 'A Contagion of Peace' in *Sojourners*, February 1982.
3. Duncan Campbell, 'When the Bombs Drop' in *Britain and The Bomb* (New Statesman, 1980), 56.
4. Ibid., 59.
5. Ibid., 59.
6. Jeff McMahan, *British Nuclear Weapons, For and Against* (Junction Books Ltd., 1981), 75.
7. Phil Bolsover, *Civil Defence: The Cruellest Confidence Trick (CND, 1980)*, 63.

Critique of Present Policies

A Nuclear Defence Policy
Is It Leading to War?

We have already sketched the transition that has taken place in the theory of deterrence. Although counter-city strikes are still part of the repertoire of the nuclear powers, the emphasis has shifted to counterforce – the ability to destroy the enemy's military capability. This is a de-stabilising development since war can start not only through a nation's ambitions to expand but through her fear of being attacked. As both sides approach the position of being able to execute a 'disarming first strike', the instability becomes greater with the increasing sense of threat experienced by both sides.

At *any* stage in the history of nuclear weapons a war through accident, miscalculation or misjudgement has been a real possibility. As Herman Kahn (the strategist who conceived of 'the ladder of escalation') has written of the early 1960's, 'it was an accident that an accident did not happen'. But the counterforce development and the move to a first strike capability creates the need for 'hair trigger' responses which must greatly increase the probability of war.

International Tension

The nuclear threat creates a dangerous climate in international affairs. The horror and immediacy of a threat to wreak nuclear devastation on another land cannot but create hostility, fear and mistrust. The 'cold-war' tension of the 1950's which may now be returning is due in large part to nuclear rivalry and threat. In such an atmosphere positions become entrenched and problems which could be resolved by negotiation become intractable. If a serious crisis arises, the intentions of the opponent are assumed to be hostile.

A number of measures have been introduced to allow for rapid communication in a crisis, such as the 'Hot-Line' telephone link between the US president and the premier of the USSR. This arrangement was agreed after the Cuban missile crisis in which the world stood on the brink of nuclear war. It is clearly a beneficial agreement, but a serious doubt must hang over its effectiveness as a last minute measure at a time of crisis. As Roger Molander* says in his article 'How I Learned to Start Worrying About Nukes':

'Ah, yes, the Hot Line. How many people know that it is a slow teletype machine, and that its use suffers from the usual problem of getting a good translation? I had witnessed two incidents in the SALT negotiations in which the United States and the Soviet Union had profoundly misunderstood each other in this fashion. The first was at Vladivostok in 1974, when President Ford and Secretary Kissinger had come home in triumph with an agreement that was found to be no agreement at all when the sides tried to write it down in agreed language. A similar incident took place in the early months of the Carter administration, when an agreement on limiting new types of ICBMs evaporated into thin air over a language disagreement. What if one of these "misunderstandings" took place in a crisis as the sides tried to control further escalation, rather than in the midst of a seven-year negotiation?'[1]

Besides, if either side were convinced of the hostile, aggressive intent of the other, the Hot Line might well be ignored, decisions being made according to what the opponent appears to be *doing*, not what he is saying.

International relations are further affected by a particular irony of the nuclear age: if fear and mistrust of the enemy is not there, then it must be manufactured. In order to rally popular support for the threat to use nuclear weapons, the enemy must be presented in fearsome terms. A horrific threat requires a horrific enemy, powerful and of evil intent. On several notable oc-

> 'In order to make the country bear the burden (of arms expenditure) we have to create an emotional atmosphere akin to wartime psychology. We must create the idea of a threat from without.'
>
> John Foster Dulles
> U.S. Secretary of State

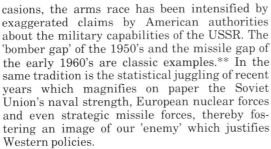

casions, the arms race has been intensified by exaggerated claims by American authorities about the military capabilities of the USSR. The 'bomber gap' of the 1950's and the missile gap of the early 1960's are classic examples.** In the same tradition is the statistical juggling of recent years which magnifies on paper the Soviet Union's naval strength, European nuclear forces and even strategic missile forces, thereby fostering an image of our 'enemy' which justifies Western policies.

Nuclear Proliferation

Another significant way in which current defence policies create conditions for nuclear war is by means of nuclear proliferation. More and more countries have, or will very soon have, the means to build their own nuclear weapons. Alva Myrdal, Sweden's former minister of disarmament, and joint-winner of the 1982 Nobel Peace Prize, suggests that one of the main driving forces behind the process of proliferation is the *symbolic* value of nuclear weapons.[2] The reliance on nuclear weapons for security and status must create the conditions whereby weaker powers will seek a nuclear capability.

Of the many problems posed by proliferation the most serious is that deterrence is basically a bi-polar game which cannot be played in a multi-polar world. Yet more and more states are acquiring nuclear weapons and the probability of nuclear war breaking out at some point on the globe is correspondingly increasing.

In conclusion, the chief factors which contribute to the increasing risk of nuclear war may be summarised as follows:
1) the development of counterforce which increases the possibility of war starting through fear of being attacked; 2) the intensification of cold war hostility which could lead to war or close off other ways of solving problems; 3) the great respect for nuclear weapons as symbols of status and power, which motivates nuclear proliferation and thus creates an increasingly unstable world situation. These are some of the aspects of our reliance on nuclear weapons which give greatest concern. (continued in study session 5)

---

* Roger Molander – a former White House nuclear strategist for the National Security Council. Now executive director of 'Ground Zero', a nuclear war education project.

** see p.47

Questions for Study and Discussion
Civil Defence

1. 'You cannot save yourself on nuclear doomsday by sitting in a fallout refuge. You are your own civil defence. Your defence is action against the policy that makes you a target.' How do you respond to this statement? Do you agree with it? If you do, what action would you take?

2. Are you aware of your council's position with regard to being a Nuclear Free Zone? Do you think it important to pursue non-co-operation with the Government's civil defence exercises? If so, how could you (or your group) be involved in this?

Critique of Present Policies
A Nuclear Defence Policy – Is It Leading to War?

3. What are the main factors in the present nuclear defence policy which are cited as increasing the likelihood of war? Do you agree that these factors are contributing to the tensions between East and West? What do you think can be done to lessen these tensions?

4. Imagine yourself as a person in a Third World country. How would you respond to the developed world's concern that you not develop nuclear weapons? (You might wish to present your ideas in the form of a letter to a leader of a developed country.)

Notes: Critique of Present Policies
A Nuclear Defence Policy – Is It Leading To War?
1. Roger Molander, 'How I Learned to Start Worrying About Nukes', *International Herald Tribune*, 25 March 1982.
2. Alva Myrdal, *The Game of Disarmament* (Spokesman, 1980).

Let us promise our fellow human beings that we will work untiringly for DISARMAMENT and the banishing of all NUCLEAR WEAPONS

POPE JOHN PAUL II AT HIROSHIMA FEB. 25 1981

44

Critique of Present Policies (Cont'd)

Arms Control Negotiations – Are They Leading To Peace?

With the risk of war increasing any hopes for improvement within the present order must lie in the forum of arms control negotiation. In fact there is little cause here for optimism. Of the eight main treaties or conventions agreed between 1963 and 1977 only one, the 1972 Biological Weapons Convention, has been a true disarmament measure, involving the renunciation of weapons which already existed. The other agreements are generally recognised to be peripheral to the arms race, leaving alone practices or weapons which really matter to either side.[1]

The 1971 Sea-Bed Treaty is an example. This treaty prohibits the placing of nuclear weapons on the sea bed. This is not a significant limitation because fixed devices are vulnerable to attack and the main interest in the sea is as an environment for *mobile* submarines carrying nuclear missiles. The Sea-Bed Treaty has been likened to a treaty that forbids the bolting of aircraft to the runway!

The SALT (Strategic Arms Limitation Talks) agreements between the US and the USSR have also failed to halt or slow down the arms race. Under the 1972 SALT I agreement anti-ballistic missile defences were limited to two sites each side, but there was in any case little hope that it was possible to develop this technology effectively. An upper limit was placed on the number of strategic missiles each side could have. But no limit was imposed on the number of warheads carried by each missile, nor on any technological innovations which might be made, and these were the areas of real interest to the superpowers. SALT II, which has never been ratified by the USA, did place limits on the number of warheads as well as on the number of missiles and long range bombers. But again the levels were very high and allowed the next stage of the arms race to proceed. These agreements did not concern non-strategic*, tactical* or theatre* nuclear weapons.

The Mutual and Balanced Force Reduction (MBFR) talks between NATO and the Warsaw Pact have been going on since 1973 and have sought agreement on reductions in the European forces (which include tactical nuclear weapons). Those have so far produced no results. The two sides have been unable to agree what sort of reductions would create a balance.

The net result of decades of negotiations over nuclear weapons is that not a single warhead has been scrapped and not a single promising avenue of weapons development has been closed off. The arms race continues at every level: in numbers of missiles and warheads; in accuracy; in satellite surveillance and communication; in anti-satellite satellites; in land, air and submarine-launched missiles; in anti-submarine warfare; in theatre, intermediate and long range systems; in neutron bombs and Cruise missiles; in computer technology for re-targeting and launching missiles ... The explanation for this seems to lie in the lack of political will to see through real measures of disarmament.

The fact that there is no intention to disarm can be seen in the political attitude to disarmament talks. Outwardly, at least in the US, officials have felt the need to describe arms control agreements in terms of advantage to their side and disadvantage to the other. Henry Kissinger has said that the SALT I agreements of 1972 allowed the USA to overcome a disadvantage in strategic forces (which did not in fact exist) by freezing overall force levels on both sides.[2] Dan Smith describes how the advocates for the SALT II agreements in 1979 argued more on the basis that they improved 'national security' by the way

* see glossary, p.116

in which they were disadvantageous to the USSR rather than that they would lead to disarmament.[3] President Nixon on his return from signing the SALT I agreement gave an indication of the spirit in which he viewed it.

'No power on earth is stronger than the USA today. None will be stronger than the USA in the future. This is the only national defence posture which can ever be acceptable to the USA.'[4]

As Smith points out this view of arms control negotiations as a search for advantage rather than disarmament does little to prepare the way for disarmament.

Another attitude towards arms control which is openly expressed is that it serves to keep the population and allied governments in accord with new military developments. An example of this attitude can be seen in the NATO decision of December 1979 to 'modernise' its European theatre nuclear forces by the introduction of Cruise and Pershing II missiles. It was seen as politically necessary to hold arms control negotiations with the USSR in parallel with the deployment of new weapons. The following description of the purpose of the talks is taken from a statement which establishes the official view of the US government:

'The general aversion to nuclear weapons that existed among important sections of public opinion in several European countries was also an important factor in the evolution of an arms control approach. The arms control element was considered essential in order to gain parliamentary and public support for the NATO proposals in several countries, particularly those where the system would be based.'[5]

In practice, as well as in theory, the approach to arms control can be seen to involve no interest in disarmament. The negotiations surrounding a ban on the testing of nuclear explosives are a case in point. A comprehensive ban on all nuclear explosions would be a major step in bringing the arms race to a halt. By 1962 negotiations between the USA and the USSR on this issue had been going on for five years. The Cuban Crisis of that year alarmed people with the realisation that nuclear war was a real possibility and Kennedy and Krushchev agreed to hurry along a ban on nuclear testing in order to reassure their peoples. The negotiations had been foundering on

the question of how to verify that neither side was conducting nuclear tests. In addition to seismic monitoring the USA insisted on having a small number of 'on-site' inspections. The USSR initially rejected this, then made the surprising concession of offering to allow three per year. The USA then insisted on seven, despite the triviality of this difference. The two sides then refused to shift from their positions and shortly thereafter agreed and signed the Partial Test Ban Treaty. This treaty bans only atmospheric tests and permits underground nuclear testing. As a disarmament measure it is valueless; both sides went on to test nuclear weapons more frequently than before. (The combined rate was 46 explosions on average per year after the treaty as compared with 27 before it.)[6] Indeed, it is probably true to say that the treaty is worse than valueless because it did succeed in calming public anxiety and thereby reducing pressure for disarmament. It seems fair to conclude that neither side actually wished to come to an agreement on the comprehensive test ban and the negotiating positions were designed to ensure that agreement could not be reached.

Arms control agreements have permitted each new stage of the arms race to proceed apace, and can be seen as positively harmful for disarmament in that they 'manage' the arms race, making it appear controlled and acceptable.[6]

In conclusion, arms control as it is practised is a very different thing from disarmament. It has been used by both sides to seek advantage, and it is used to pacify governments and people who are anxious about the arms race. Negotiations for genuine *reduction* of forces will only succeed when the will to succeed is genuine on the part of governments.

Statistics: Their Use and Abuse

Since nations do not declare their genuine intentions to their competitors it is a tenet of defence planning that the opponent's intentions are gauged not by its words but by its actions. The degree of threat that it presents is assessed by the number of missiles, tanks, ships or aeroplanes it is building and by where it is deploying them.

Inevitably this data has become ammunition in the propaganda war between the two sides in the arms race. As pointed out earlier, it is necessary to justify the spiral of expenditure on arms programmes by portraying the enemy as threatening and powerful. In the West the main sources of

'I can go into my office, pick up the telephone and in 25 minutes 70 million people will be dead.'
Richard Nixon

information about Warsaw Pact strength are US government intelligence agencies, which are closely identified with the interests of the US defence establishment. It is not, therefore, surprising that much of the data that is presented to the public has been filtered to add a particular slant to the picture of the Soviet threat in the public mind.[7]

Examples of this process abound – at present we hear a lot about the Soviet naval build up. The Soviet Navy, however, has fewer ships than in 1958 and is scrapping ships faster than it is building them. The proportion of old ships in the Soviet Navy is greater now than in 1958 and the USSR has lower naval construction rates than the NATO states. The Soviet naval 'build up' has not occurred and is not occurring. What is happening is that the Soviet Navy is being deployed in areas such as the Mediterranean and the Indian Ocean into which it did not venture in the 1950's and early 1960's.[8]

Another classic example of the use of 'misinformation' was the scare of the 'missile gap' in the USA in the early 1960's. As Robert Neild recounts it:[9]

'The missile gap occurred after the Russians

had achieved a technical breakthrough in 1957 by putting up Sputnik ... Huge estimates of the future number of Soviet missiles were circulated and attacks were made on the Eisenhower government for neglecting the nation's defences ... In Table 1 the projection of inter-continental ballistic missile (ICBM) numbers published by Joseph Alsop, the columnist, who was the chief spokesman of the alarmists within the military establishment, is compared with the actual number of ICBMs as later acknowledged in the West ...

Table 1
Missile gap: ICBMs
A *Missile Gap Projection*

	USA	USSR	Balance
1960	30	100	−70
1961	70	500	−430
1962	130	1000	870
1963	130	1500	−1370
1964	130	2000	−1870

B *'Actual' figures*

	USA	USSR	Balance
1960	18	4	+14
1961	63	20	+43
1962	294	75	+219
1963	424	100	+324
1964	834	200	+634

Balance:
(+ = US superiority)
(− = Soviet superiority)

'In a post-mortem on the episode, Senator Symington, ... stated that the high figure for Soviet missile strength was an intelligence estimate of the "theoretical" Soviet capability ... He complained that on the basis of the wrong figures he and other American leaders were caused to believe that there was a missile gap.'

In the midst of the confusion caused by this sort of misinformation several points are clear.
1. Both the USSR and the USA are militarily very powerful and show no inclination towards slowing the arms race.
2. The Warsaw Pact is generally agreed to have larger numbers of most categories of con-

ventional arms (tanks, aircraft, etc.). The quality of these arms is, however, very considerably lower than those of NATO.

3. In terms of nuclear weapons there is probably rough parity between the strategic forces of the USA and those of the USSR. Both sides lead in some aspects and neither could expect to win a war. In Europe NATO has a greater number of short range nuclear forces. Again, these comparisons cannot easily be interpreted in terms of military advantage.

4. Despite public pronouncements to the contrary NATO seems to be generally content with the balance of military power in Europe. As Dan Smith points out:[10] 'In 1975, NATO ministers reportedly agreed that NATO did not face conventional inferiority and had more combat-ready soldiers in Europe than the Warsaw Pact' and 'In his 1978 report, the Chairman of the Joint Chiefs of Staff, after page upon page apparently bewailing American disadvantage, noted that "Science and technology have been among the principal factors in continued overall US military superiority"'.

5. While the 'facts' about relative military strengths are always in doubt, and there are no independent spy satellites to provide data free of the influence of Moscow or Washington,

there are three sources that are generally agreed to be useful. These are:
(i)   The year books and other publications of the Stockholm International Peace Research Institute (SIPRI).
(ii) 'The Military Balance' published annually by the International Institute of Strategic Studies in London.
(iii) The series of 'Jane's' annuals which provide technical and other details.

6. The data for nuclear weapons below seems to be generally agreed:

Strategic Nuclear Forces (1981)[12]

	USA	USSR
Total of Bombers and Missiles	2.000	2.504
Total of Bombs and Warheads	9.000	7.000

Nuclear Weapons (short and long-range) in European Theatre[13]

	NATO	Warsaw Pact
Total of Bombs and Warheads	ca. 7.500	ca. 3.500

Notes: Critique of Present Policies (contd)
Arms Control Negotiations – Are They Leading To Peace?
1. Robert Neild, *How To Make Up Your Mind About The Bomb* (André Deutsch, 1981), 73-75. *World Armaments and Disarmament, SIPRI Yearbook 1981* (Taylor and Francis, 1981), ch.13.
2. Dan Smith, *The Defence of the Realm in the 1980's* (Croom Helm, 1980), 219.
3. Ibid.
4. President Nixon quoted in Myrdal, *The Game of Disarmament (Spokesman, 1976)*, 25.
5. US Library of Congress Research Service, 'The Evolution of NATO's Decision to "Modernise" Theatre Nuclear Weapons', in Alva Myrdal and others, *Dynamics of European Nuclear Disarmament* (Spokesman, 1981), 98.
6. *SIPRI Yearbook 1981*, 373.
7. Myrdal, *The Game of Disarmament*, 107.
8. Dan Smith, *The Defence of the Realm in the 1980's*, ch.4.
9. Ibid., 50-51.
10. Robert Neild, *How To Make Up Your Mind About the Bomb*, 24, 25.
11. Dan Smith, *The Defence of the Realm in the 1980's*, 71.
12. Stockholm International Peace Research Institute, *1981 Year Book*, 275-276.
13. Dan Smith, 'The European Nuclear Theatre', in E. P. Thompson and D. Smith, eds., *Protest and Survive* (Penguin, 1980), 112, 124.

Changes in Direction

Having looked at Britain's present defence policy we see much that concerns us. But are there alternatives? It often seems that there are not. We live in a real world where nations with military strength regularly invade weaker ones. Military force is, unfortunately, a very real component in the relationship between different states. Given this fact, some defence policy is advisable for governments.

In formulating a defence policy choices have to be made between emphasising saving the state and government, or saving the lives of the civilian population. Too many people it seems almost inevitable that the interests of governments will differ from the interests of their subjects. Depending on its priorities, a country's military action can vary greatly. It can 'fly the flag' around the world, defend the state from external invasion, defend the government from internal insurrection, or wage nuclear war from deep bunkers at the expense of the lives of the civilian population.

Looking realistically at Britain's situation there are several possible non-nuclear defence policies open to us.[1] We could adopt a policy similar to that of other non-nuclear states in NATO; that is to stay under the American nuclear umbrella but spend the money allotted to Polaris on conventional arms. This is the kind of policy that has been adopted by Canada.

At the other end of the scale, we could adopt a policy of non-violent resistance to an invading army.[2] This latter policy, which by means of systematic and sacrificial non-cooperation would deprive an invader of his capacity to govern, is more feasible than it sounds. Throughout history much of the most effective resistance to oppression has been carried out by means of non-violent resistance. And in the nuclear age it may be the only real way to defend a nation. This was the conclusion of the greatest British strategic thinker of our century, Sir Basil Liddell-Hart,

who wrote in 1967: 'It is necessary to demonstrate that [non-violent civilian defence] is a workable policy, and that it is more workable than military defence.'[2] 'National defence through passive resistance' is also the mature position of George Kennan, the great American Christian diplomat and Sovietologist who was the architect of 'containment'.

A policy somewhere between these two extremes is suggested by Dan Smith. In *The Defence of the Realm in the 1980's* he argues for a defence policy almost exclusively concerned with repulsing a military attack on British soil. He suggests that to a large extent current policies are based on the notion that Britain is a great power acting out a world role, a notion that he sees as neither true nor desirable. Rather than following our present strategy of 'retaliatory deterrence' based upon nuclear weapons, he suggests scrapping our nuclear weapons, renouncing the American nuclear 'umbrella', removing American bases in Britain, (bases which form the majority of nuclear targets in this country), and developing a strategy which he calls 'defensive deterrence'.

This strategy is similar to that followed by Sweden, Switzerland and Yugoslavia. It involves having strong armed forces based on our own territory, armed with conventional weapons appropriate to defence – for example, armed with many cheap anti-tank and anti-aircraft weapons rather than a few expensive tanks or long range bombers. In this way aggressors are deterred from invasion by the prospect of extremely heavy military losses. Dan Smith suggests that this policy would involve Britain withdrawing at least partially from NATO. She would then be free to follow a foreign policy less dependent on US and European approval, possibly including a real commitment to disarmament.

Opponents of a non-nuclear defence policy argue that it might prove to be more expensive.

They cite Sweden as an example of a country whose defence expenditure per capita is higher than Britain's. Sweden has a strong non-nuclear military defence. Dan Smith contests this argument, suggesting that a 'defensive-deterrence' strategy would not be more expensive and may, in fact, be cheaper. He points out that Sweden has both a larger physical area and a smaller population to defend, so that a per capita comparison of defence spending is misleading.

Another argument often heard against a non-nuclear defence policy for Britain is that, if made today, such a change of policy would destabilise the balance between NATO and the Warsaw Pact thereby increasing the risk of war. This would only be true if there was a balance of forces between East and West. However, on the contrary, there is not a delicate balance but an immense amount of overkill – that is to say that each side has enough weapons already to kill everybody on the other side many times over. (By 1976 the United States possessed a nuclear stockpile of 8,000 megatons – the equivalent of 615,385 bombs like the atom bomb dropped on Hiroshima. 'Using the Hiroshima analogy the nuclear stockpile of the United States alone translates into a potential kill-power 12 times the present world population.')[3] So, subtracting the small British proportion of weapons will not significantly affect the 'balance' of forces. What may be more to the point is the question of US bases in Britain. It may be true that if Britain were to

50

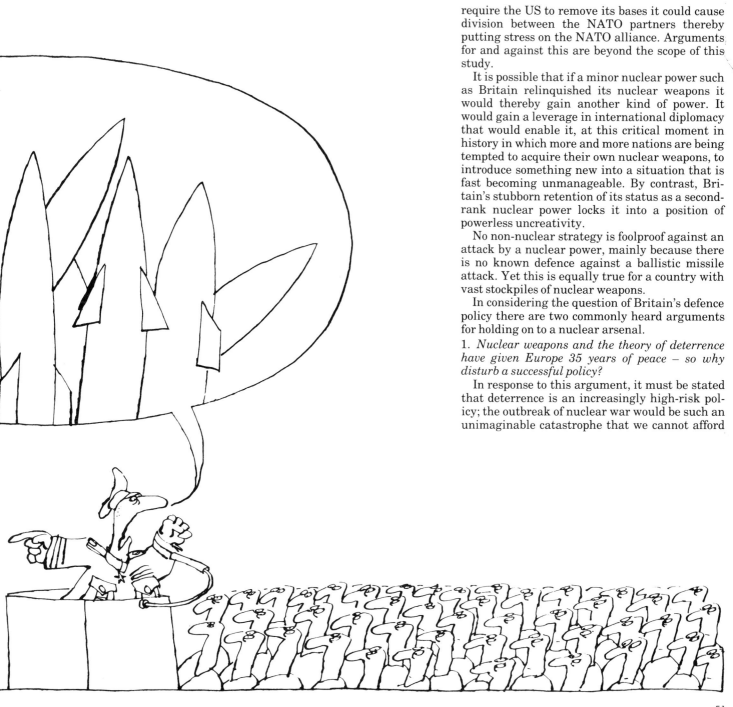

require the US to remove its bases it could cause division between the NATO partners thereby putting stress on the NATO alliance. Arguments for and against this are beyond the scope of this study.

It is possible that if a minor nuclear power such as Britain relinquished its nuclear weapons it would thereby gain another kind of power. It would gain a leverage in international diplomacy that would enable it, at this critical moment in history in which more and more nations are being tempted to acquire their own nuclear weapons, to introduce something new into a situation that is fast becoming unmanageable. By contrast, Britain's stubborn retention of its status as a second-rank nuclear power locks it into a position of powerless uncreativity.

No non-nuclear strategy is foolproof against an attack by a nuclear power, mainly because there is no known defence against a ballistic missile attack. Yet this is equally true for a country with vast stockpiles of nuclear weapons.

In considering the question of Britain's defence policy there are two commonly heard arguments for holding on to a nuclear arsenal.

1. *Nuclear weapons and the theory of deterrence have given Europe 35 years of peace – so why disturb a successful policy?*

In response to this argument, it must be stated that deterrence is an increasingly high-risk policy; the outbreak of nuclear war would be such an unimaginable catastrophe that we cannot afford the deterrence strategy to fail even once. Yet the longer we continue it, the greater the likelihood that it will fail. As we have seen, recent changes in technology and strategy have increased the risk of nuclear war. In politics the development of counterforce weapons has undermined the whole theory, since it points towards a pre-emptive first strike. This is because the only logical use of warheads targeted on one's opponents' military installations lies in using them first. There is little point in attacking empty silos! So nuclear deterrence has at best proved a temporary strategy. It must now be replaced by a strategy involving a lesser risk. Moreover, it must be pointed out that nuclear weapons have *not* deterred war. Over 140 conflicts have taken place in the Third World since the Second World War, many consisting of superpower battles fought by proxy using weapons supplied through the arms trade. Thus the battleground has shifted from Europe to the underdeveloped world, not so much because nuclear weapons have necessarily deterred war in the industrialised world, but more because the real East/West conflict (particularly over resources) lies in the Third World, not in Europe itself.

2. *World disarmament, which is surely the aim of those supporting unilateral disarmament, will never happen as you cannot take away the knowledge of how to build bombs. Even if a nation renounces its weapons, there is no guarantee that it will not rebuild its nuclear arsenals.*

It *is* impossible to prevent a nation that has disarmed from subsequently re-arming. To disarm must always involve a risk. On the other hand, if the world's most powerful nations chose to renounce nuclear weapons the pressures to re-arm would be greatly lessened. It is also possible to develop methods for verifying that nuclear weapons are not being constructed. The most important consideration is, 'What is the alternative?' To continue along our present path is to face ever-increasing risk. In the words of Harold Macmillan:

'If all this capacity for destruction is spread around the world in the hands of all kinds of different characters – dictators, reactionaries, revolutionaries, madmen – then sooner or later, and certainly I think by the end of this century, either by error or insanity, the great crime will be committed.'

Questions for Study and Discussion

Critique of Present Policies (contd)

Arms Control Negotiations – Are They Leading To Peace?

1. 'The net result of decades of negotiations over nuclear weapons is that not a single warhead has been scrapped and not a single promising avenue of weapons development has been closed off.' Discuss your response to this statement.
2. 'The arms control element was considered essential in order to gain parliamentary and public support for the NATO proposals in several countries, particularly those where the system would be based.' How do you feel about the use of arms control talks to quieten opposition to new weapons, as expressed in this quote from a US Library of Congress document?
3. In the USA currently there is a strong, grass-roots movement advocating a 'nuclear freeze' – a moratorium on the testing, production, and deployment of all new and additional nuclear weapons and weapons delivery systems. In the light of the ineffectiveness of arms control, do you think such a moratorium could be an important step in halting the arms race?
4. What changes in defence policy are advocated by Dan Smith? What is your assessment of his proposals?
5. How do you evaluate the 'risk' of disarmament as compared to the 'risk' of a nuclear war?

Notes: Changes of Direction

1. Anders Boserup, 'Nuclear Disarmament: Non-Nuclear Defence' and Ben Dankbaar, 'Alternative Defence Policies and Modern Weapon Technology' in Kalder, Smith, ed. *Disarming Europe* (Merlin, 1982).
2. B. H Liddell-Hart, 'Lessons from Resistance Movements – Guerilla and Non-Violent', in Adam Roberts, ed., *The Strategy of Civilian Defence* (Faber & Faber, 1967), 205-211.
   George Urban, 'From Containment to Self-Containment: A Conversation with George Kennan', *Encounter* 47, (September 1976), 37.
   Michael Randle, 'Defence without the Bomb', *ADIU Report*, January/February 1981, 4-7, 11.
   Gene Keyes, 'Strategic Non-Violent Defense: The Construct of an Option', *Journal of Strategic Studies*, 4 (June 1981).
3. Ruth Legar Sivard quoted in *Sojourners*, February 1977.

PART II

Swords into Ploughshares

Introduction to Part Two

We are living in a dangerous world. As the previous section of this Study Guide has demonstrated, the probability of nuclear war is increasing. Weapons designed to bring security are bringing fear – and heightened insecurity. Policies which some claim have brought us 35 years of peace seem to be running out of time. And the consequences of their failure would be a global calamity which would make the Black Death of the fourteenth century, which killed one of every two Europeans, seem minor by comparison. As Christians we are called to analyse the current trends of our time; and it is our divinely-given prophetic vocation to point out what will happen if they continue. The Biblical prophets were not reclusive diviners of events in the dim future; they were public figures, keen observers of their times. And they spoke God's word which compelled their contemporaries to face the inevitable consequences of their socio-political behaviour. The church in the 1980s is called to do likewise.

But as Christians we are not speaking out against the nuclear arms policies of our governments merely because they appear a desperate gamble, or merely because the consequences of miscalculating would be 'a catastrophe unprecedented in human history'.[1] We are also opposing these policies because our Christian moral antennae are picking up danger signals. Not for centuries have Christians been as concerned about the morality of warfare as we are today. Pope John Paul II has both reflected and shaped this concern. 'War', he told us in Coventry, 'is totally unacceptable as a means of settling differences between nations'.[2] And the debate over the rightness of sending the task force in the Falklands/Malvinas war have shown that Christians in this country are thinking both subtly and courageously about war.

This thinking has been gaining in strength for some years. It is probably easiest to date its be-ginning from December 1979, when NATO foreign ministers decided to station US Cruise and Pershing II missiles in Europe. But it has been reinforced by the British decision to acquire Trident missile submarines, by the general deterioration of detente between the superpowers, and by the assertive policies and abrasive rhetoric of Margaret Thatcher and Ronald Reagan. Behind it all has been the uneasy realisation that the rules of the nuclear race are changing and that the 'balance of terror' is less stable than we had assumed.

As a result of these developments, Christians of many traditions have been thinking unprecedented thoughts. Billy Graham, for example, in 1978 had an experience in Auschwitz which for the first time gave him a gut-level appreciation of what the holocaust had been like, and what the next holocaust would be like if the bombs fell. Since this experience, which he called his 'change of heart', he has been speaking out against the arms race.[3] An astonishing proportion of the American Catholic bishops have come to share this concern as well; at least 57 US bishops have joined the Pax Christi movement, and the Archbishop of Seattle has refused to pay taxes to support nuclear weapons.[4] In the light of these developments, it is not surprising that recent authoritative studies by Anglican and Roman Catholic theologians on behalf of official bodies of their churches have recommended unilateral nuclear disarmament for Britain.[5]

So Christians are speaking out against our current nuclear policies; they are saying that these are both dangerous and wrong. They are doing so not because they are in complete agreement in their personal convictions about violence. Some, such as the well-known Methodist Dr. Kenneth Greet, are pacifists: they believe that Jesus Christ, in calling his disciples to work non-violently for justice, forbade them from taking life under any circumstances.[6] A

'... because we live in a sinful world it means we have to take something like nuclear armaments seriously. We know the terrible violence of which the human heart is capable.'

Dr Billy Graham, interview with Sojourners, August 1979

larger number, such as the Anglican church statesman John Stott, are adherents of the Just War: they believe that Christians in the pursuit of justice are allowed to take life, but only in certain carefully defined circumstances.[7] It is not surprising, therefore, that these pacifists and Just War Christians disagree on many matters – the death penalty, the Falklands/Malvinas crisis, Northern Ireland.

On the use of nuclear weapons, however, they agree.[8] Despite their disagreements in other areas, they are working together against nuclear weapons. The Christian peace movement of today is not a movement made up solely of peace activists. It is a coalition of believers of different views and backgrounds – 'Just War' adherents and pacifists, bishops and ordinary laymen, many of whom are quite surprised at themselves when they find themselves participating in a demonstration – who have been brought together by a 'grave moral evil' – the nuclear bomb.

In the pages that follow, I will attempt to guide you through the underlying assumptions and the scriptural bases of both the Just War and pacifism. Although I am a pacifist, I greatly admire the spiritual insights and intellectual integrity of many adherents of the Just War. I will therefore attempt to present the two positions as fairly as I can, in light of the thinking of their best representatives (and both positions have had some bad ones!), allowing you to make up your minds about the relative merits of both. It will become clear as I proceed why pacifists and adherents of the Just War, differing as they do about many things, can agree to condemn nuclear weapons. Indeed, as I will point out in closing, there are many common affirmations which both pacifists and Just War theorists can make, and many common actions which they can undertake. These two positions need not, therefore, be in conflict; in the nuclear age they properly belong together.

'The most faithful disciples of Christ have been builders of peace, to the point of forgiving their enemies, sometimes even to the point of giving their lives for them. Their example marks the path for a new humanity no longer content with provisional compromises but instead achieving the deepest sort of brotherhood.'

Pope John Paul II

5. Working Party for the Board for Social Responsibility of the Church of England, *The Church and the Bomb: Nuclear Weapons and Christian Conscience* (Hodder and Stoughton, 1982); Roger Ruston, O.P., *Nuclear Deterrence – Right or Wrong?* (prepared for the Commission for International Justice and Peace of England and Wales) (Catholic Information Services, 1981).
6. Kenneth Greet, *The Big Sin* (Marshall, Morgan and Scott, 1982).
7. John Stott, 'Calling for Peacemakers in a Nuclear Age', *Christianity Today,* 8 February and 7 March 1980.
8. As John Stott describes his position, 'If we are to think clearly about these issues, it is important to distinguish between the possession, the threat to use, and the actual use of nuclear weapons. I believe the use would be immoral, because of the indiscriminate effects, and therefore that the active threat to use would be equally immoral. But it is arguable that possession is not so much with a view to use as with a view to *deterring* use. Seen thus, it could not be said that possession and use are equally immoral. So nuclear pacifism does not inevitably lead to total unilateralism. Although a nuclear pacifist myself, I would go on to describe myself as a multi-lateralist, who at the same time longs for imaginative (though realistic) unilateral gestures.'

Notes: Introduction to Part II

1. US Congress, Office of Technology Assessment, *The Effects of Nuclear War* (Croom Helm, 1980), 3.
2. John Paul II, *The Pope Teaches* (Catholic Truth Society, 1982), 170.
3. Billy Graham, 'A Change of Heart', *Sojourners,* August 1979, 12-14.
4. 'A Blast from the Bishops', *Time,* 8 November 1982, 21; Archbishop Raymond Hunthausen, pastoral letter of January 1982, printed in *Sojourners,* March 1982, 7.

The Just War Doctrine

Because the Just War doctrine has been the official teaching of the major Western Christian traditions (Catholic, Anglican, Lutheran, and Reformed) since the fifth century A.D., we shall begin with it.[1]

The Just War doctrine has never been fixed and unchanging. Since its beginning in the writings of Saints Ambrose and Augustine, it has developed gradually, changing in response to new experiences and insights. But in every era, thinkers within the Just War tradition have professed a common aim – to limit war in the pursuit of justice. Christians must therefore never take life, unless certain conditions are met.

Undergirding the Just War tradition are certain assumptions.

1. Because this world is marred by the Fall, Christians cannot escape from evil, which expresses itself in selfishness and greed and which leads to conflict.

2. War is therefore an unavoidable part of human experience. It is evil; in fact, it is so evil that, as selfish parties unjustly pursue their self-interest, it tends to escalate uncontrollably.

3. War can, however, be controlled. Evil though it is, it can be limited so that it is a *lesser evil,* a means of stopping a greater evil and of preserving justice. To limit war in this way there must be rules, which safeguard justice and which prevent violence from getting out of hand.

4. These rules ('the Just War conditions') only apply to official, government-level violence, for only official violence can be even-handed and judicial enough to be an expression of justice. The violence of private individuals, on the other hand, tends to be marked by unjudicial hatred, fear and anger; therefore it is ruled out by the Just War doctrine. Only at the command of the government can the individual legitimately take life. The Just War conditions have changed greatly over the past fifteen hundred years. Even today it is impossible to come up with a list of conditions which all theologians will accept. But the following conditions are on the lists of most thinkers, and are a reasonable basis for our discussion.[2] They assert that it is possible for a Christian to fight justly if: a) his cause is just; b) he uses only just means; c) his intention (attitude) is right; and d) he disobeys if he is asked to do anything which goes contrary to any of the above. Let us examine these in turn.

1. Just Cause: There are certain offences against justice which governments, acting as policemen of the international order, must set right, if necessary by armed force. They will resort to military action with great reluctance:

'The wise man, they say, will wage just wars. Surely, if he remembers that he is a human being, he will rather lament the fact that he is faced with the necessity of waging just wars; for if they were not just, he would not have to engage in them, and consequently there would be no wars for a wise man. For it is the injustice of the opposing side that lays on the wise man the duty of waging wars ...'

(Augustine, *City of God*, XIX, 7)

In a just cause, there will be

a. a *clear wrong,* such as an unprovoked attack by an aggressor, which will be met by force to restore the just situation which has been disturbed. Only a defensive war can be a Just War.

b. resort to violence only as a *last resort.* Only after all negotiations and compromises have been tried and failed must there be recourse to armed force.

c. declaration of war by a *legitimate authority*. Military action is the right of governments, not of private individuals or unofficial bodies.

d. *limited objectives*. The aim of war is to set right a recognised wrong and thereby to restore *peace*. War is thus a limited exercise in forceful peacemaking, and is incompatible with an attempt to destroy the enemy's economy, government or ideology.

2. Just Means: These are an important as the *just cause* if the war is to be a Just War. For it is possible to respond to one injustice in such a grossly destructive fashion that the cause of justice is set back, making the situation even worse than it would have been if there had been no war at all and no attempt had been made to correct the original injustice. Unless a Just War is being fought justly, it thus becomes an *unjust war,* and killing in it becomes murder. The means used in waging a just war must therefore be

a. *proportionate:* No more violence must be used than is in keeping with the limited objective of a just peace, and than is warranted by the original injustice. This rules out total or unlimited warfare.

'Inasmuch as wars ought to be waged for the common good, if some one city cannot be recaptured without greater evils befalling the State, such as the devastation of many cities, great slaughter of human beings, provocation of princes, occasions for new wars ... it is indubitable that the prince is bound rather to give up his own rights and abstain from war.'

(Vitoria, *De Indis* [1540], sect. 33)

b. *discriminate:* there must be *noncombatant immunity.* Violence must be directed only against enemy soldiers and munition workers, not against civilians, women and children. At times noncombatants will unfortunately be hit; this is morally tolerable if the intended targets were military. According to this 'double effect' reasoning, the civilian dead are 'unintended collateral casualties' for whom no one is morally responsible.

3. Right Intention: Amidst the unavoidable action of killing, one must 'cherish the spirit of a peacemaker', avoiding hatred, greed and brutality.[3] Although outwardly one is acting severely, inwardly one must have a disposition of heart towards the enemy that is loving.

4. Obligation to Just Disobedience (the 'Nuremberg principle'): Ever since Luther and Vitoria in the sixteenth century, theologians have insisted that it is the duty of soldiers to disobey their commanders rather than fight in an unjust cause or use unjust means. The victorious Allies gave expression to this principle in the trials which were held after World War II in

The sophistication of war technology increases: The Long Wittenham bronze shield. A rare piece of military equipment from the end of the second millennium BC.

Nuremberg and Tokyo of German and Japanese 'war criminals'.

These then are the conditions which Just War thinkers have used to justify the violence of warfare. The effectiveness of these conditions in situations of conflict is questionable, but the fact that they have become the basis of the international law of war is an indicator of their influence. They represent the dominant Christian tradition of thinking about the morality of warfare; we must treat them with respect.

It is not surprising that the Just War conditions do not readily flow from Scripture. St. Augustine drew many of them from the pagan writers of the ancient world, especially Cicero; and the Greek philosopher Aristotle was the first person to use the term 'just war'.[4] To Just War thinkers this is not worrisome; indeed it is a strength. For Scripture and secular insight are not necessarily in conflict. There is, they affirm, a *natural law* written in the hearts of men and women (Rom. 1-3) and embedded in the created order, which is in keeping with the divine law of Scripture. Nevertheless, from the time of their adoption of the Just War theory in the fifth century, theologians have sought to provide a biblical basis for it.[5]

In both Old and New Testaments, Just War thinkers argue, God is revealed to be a God of justice and peace. Both of these are expressions of his love, which is perfect and beyond human understanding. There can thus be no genuine conflict between his love and justice, or between his justice and his peace. All of these are mutually compatible expressions of each other, and only unbiblical thinking can drive wedges between them.

1. *God established government for justice.* In the *Old Testament,* God showed his loving concern for justice and peace in society by instituting government which he empowered to use force to restrict and punish evil. In the Law at least ten crimes are listed as deserving capital punishment. By extrapolation from this domestic justice, it is inferred that God desires governments to function as instruments of his justice on the international level as well, if necessary by using military force.

2. *God commanded nations to wage war.* Wars of judgement and wars of conquest were both fought at the express order of God. War is therefore clearly on some occasion in keeping with his will. In fact, the Old Testament writers call Yahweh 'a man of war' and the 'Lord of hosts (armies)' (e.g. Exo. 15:3; Ps. 24:8-10).

3. *God often praised warriors.* King David, for example, was 'a man after (God's) own heart' (I Sam. 13:14). And the psalmist rejoiced in God 'who trains my hands for war, and my fingers for battle' (Ps. 144:1).

4. *God was concerned to limit violence.* Despite his authorisation of governmental violence, God sought to limit it by
a. making it *proportionate.* The Law restricts permissible violence to retribution in kind. There

Section of the Bayeux tapestry showing William about to defeat Harold at the Battle of Hastings in 1066.

shall be no more than *one* eye for an eye (Exo. 21:24).

b. making it *discriminate*. Throughout the Old Testament God showed a passionate concern for the protection of innocent people. The Lord 'hates hands that shed innocent blood' (Prov. 6:16-17), for life is his gift and may not be taken away except by his authority. Therefore the Law commanded, 'Do not slay the innocent and righteous' (Exo. 23:7). Cities of refuge were established 'lest innocent blood be shed' (Deut. 19:10). When going to war against neighbouring nations, Israel was instructed to spare 'the women and the little ones' (Deut. 20:14). Nations which made 'haste to shed innocent blood' came under his judgement (Isa. 59:7). Indeed, filling a capital city with innocent blood was a sin which 'the Lord would not pardon' (2 Kings 24:4).

c. urging a *peaceful settlement* before battle. When Israel drew near to a city to fight against it, they were to 'offer terms of peace to it' (Deut. 20:10).

5. The Old Testament *mourns the violence of war* and anticipates its eradication. The psalmists longed for peace (Ps. 46:9; 120:6-7); the prophets denounced the atrocities of warfare (Amos 1-2); and there was an anticipation of the day when God's law would be triumphant and peace would hold universal sway (Micah 4:1-4).

The *New Testament* fulfills the Old Testament. But, Just War thinkers argue, it cannot be in contradiction to it, for the God and Father of Jesus Christ is also the God of Abraham, Isaac and Jacob (Matt. 22:32). It is not surprising, therefore, that Just War thinkers find New Testament teaching on warfare, although less explicit than that of the Old Testament, to be in agreement with it.

1. *John the Baptist's instructions*. When soldiers came repentantly to John, he did not tell them to leave their profession; he admonished them to be just in their military conduct (Luke 3:14).

2. *Soldiers occur in a favourable light*. Jesus commended the faith of a centurion (Matt. 8:11-12); and the centurion Cornelius was the first Gentile believer (Acts 10). In neither case, according to the biblical record, was the soldier told to leave his job.

3. *Render to Caesar*. Jesus taught his disciples to be obedient to the government except when its orders conflict with God's will (Matt. 22:21). This obedience includes the payment of taxes, a portion of which will go to support the armed forces. Although Jesus told his disciples not to fight to protect him (Jn. 18:36), he was merely prohibiting the use of military force for *religious* causes; he also was safeguarding his God-given mission to die on the cross.

4. *Love your enemies*. This teaching (Matt. 5:45; Luke 6:27) must be read in the context of the other biblical passages. When Jesus spoke these words, Just War thinkers contend, he probably did not have in mind warfare (conflict with collective, national enemies). He was rather instructing his disciples that they should deal lovingly with their individual enemies and persecutors. But even if Jesus had been thinking of situations of military conflict, he was not forbidding his disciples to take life; he was admonishing them to have an *attitude/intention of love* toward the enemies whom they unfortunately were required to kill.

5. *Love your neighbour*. In the parable of the Good Samaritan (Luke 10:29-37), Jesus commended the Samaritan who showed himself to be a neighbour by serving the victim of armed robbery. Jesus did not tell his disciples, however, what the Samaritan would have done if he had come upon the scene while the victim was being mugged. Just War thinkers argue that neighbour-love (Luke 10:27) would have compelled the Samaritan forcibly to resist the attackers. The biblical view of violence requires action to protect, not oneself, but innocent victims (the 'third party').

6. *Jesus resisted evil*. In his sharp words to the Pharisees (Matt. 23) and in his cleansing of the Temple (John 2:13 ff.) Jesus engaged in vigorous acts of resistance, to the point of resorting to physical violence (the whip). Therefore his teaching, 'Do not resist one who is evil' (Matt. 5:39) must be an example of colourful Jewish exaggeration; it cannot mean that his disciples should be non-resistant or passive in the face of evil.

7. *Romans 13:1-7*. This key passage, according to Just War thinkers, summarises the message of both testaments concerning the use of violent means by governments. God has established governments to be his servants, wielding the sword to restrain and punish evildoers (cf. 1 Peter 2:13-14). Although Romans 13 applies directly only to domestic order and criminal justice, by extrapolation it would also seem to apply to in-

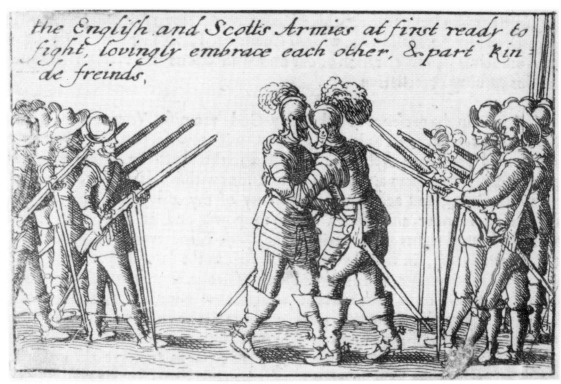

the English and Scotts Armies at first ready to fight, lovingly embrace each other, & part kinde freinds,

Charles I forced to accept the establishment of Presbyterian Church government in Scotland through the success of the Covenanters' invasion of England in 1640.

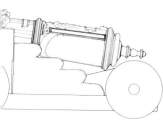

ternational relations. Governments would thus be commissioned to use military force to preserve justice and to punish those nations which disturb it. This passage does not specify how Christian believers should behave. But its admonition to 'be subject' would seem to imply that we must fight in a just international conflict if the government orders us to do so. On the other hand, if the government calls us to fight in a war that is unjust, we Christians would not seem to be required to obey. Indeed, we would be called to resist the unjust order ('We must obey God rather than man' [Acts 5:29]).

Just War thinkers thus argue strongly against the position of pacifist Christians. It is the duty of Christians to take life, Just War theorists maintain, but only under certain carefully specified circumstances; pacifists, who deny that there are ever such circumstances, they find to be unbiblically idealistic. A leading British Christian philosopher in the Just War tradition has put it like this:

'Christianity is a severe and practicable religion, not a beautifully ideal but impracticable one. Its moral precepts, [except for the stricter laws about marriage which Christ enacted, abrogating some of the permissions of the Old Law], are those of the Old Testament; and its God is the God of Israel.'[6]

But although the Just War doctrine can justify warfare, it is not meant to be a means of blessing whatever warlike acts the government of the moment is determined to make. It is meant to be a reference standard. Its rules have been formulated to assist believers in deciding whether a given war is just and thus whether their participation in it can be justified.

A Just War is thus not any war; and it cannot be total war. It is only a war in which it is clear which government is in the wrong, in which it is clear that the evil to which the war is a response is greater than the evil which the war itself

British marines as part of the invasion forces fighting at Gallipoli in 1915, photographed from the monument to the marines in The Mall, London.

would bring about, in which the innocent non-combatants are not being wilfully or knowingly killed, and in which, because the combatants are maintaining a loving intention in their hearts, the enemy is not being dehumanised. If the war fails to meet any of these conditions, Christians must recognise that they are crossing a moral boundary line – the line which divides war from murder. At that moment, the Just War doctrine calls on Christian statesmen to desist and Christian soldiers to disobey.

As technology has advanced, wars have increasingly tended to cross that boundary line. This has especially been so in the Twentieth Century. In the Vietnam War, for example, the vast firepower of the United States ensured that ten civilians were killed for every military fatality. And in Europe during World War II, the Allied air forces pursued a policy of the area bombing of German cities, intentionally killing over 580,000 civilians.[7] This policy was manifestly against

Just War teaching which requires noncombatant immunity. But only one prominent English Christian spokesman, Bishop George Bell of Chichester, spoke out against it; and he for his pains, was for a time forbidden to preach in his own cathedral![8]

The destructive power of 'conventional' weapons is thus truly vast, but it is still theoretically possible to use them in a discriminate way that will almost completely spare the noncombatants. With nuclear weapons such discrimination is no longer possible. Einstein commented that 'the unleashed power of the atom has changed everything but our way of thinking'.[9] It certainly has changed the nature of warfare. Because of the tremendous destructive power of nuclear weapons, because of their radiation and fallout, because of the probability of escalation and the problems of command and control, nuclear weapons are a new phenomenon in the history of warfare.

(Opposite) Sophisticated ammunition for sale, on display at the Farnborough Air Show in 1982.

> **'Every gun that is made, every warship that is launched, every rocket fired signifies a theft from those that hunger and are not fed, from those who are cold and are not clothed.'**
>
> President Eisenhower

They are intrinsically indiscriminate. Only the most implausible of scenarios conceives of their use without the foreseen deaths of millions of civilians. In a hypothetical limited 'counter-force' war in which only military targets would be attacked, the casualty toll would be in the tens of millions. And responsible observers, such as the late Lord Mountbatten, are convinced that such a 'limited war' could not remain limited; if it did so, it would be – in the judgement of the International Institute for Strategic Studies – a 'miracle'.[10] Far more likely is rapid escalation to all-out nuclear war, with the toll of prompt casualties in

the hundreds of millions.

As a result of the monstrous destructive power of these weapons, Just War thinkers are in a difficult position. For the first time in history the logic of their convictions is compelling them to renounce a weapons system rather than to accommodate it. Not surprisingly, some of them have found this difficult. An eminent American academic, Paul Ramsey, has taken comfort that in a 'counter-force' nuclear war as few as 25 million civilians might be killed; and since their deaths would be the anticipated but not 'intended' side-effects of missiles aimed at military targets, the attackers would be morally blameless.[11] Other thinkers in the Just War tradition have argued that nuclear weapons, despite the fact that our readiness to use them must be 'infinitely credible' and they can be fired on a few minutes' notice, exist only as a deterrent. There is nothing immoral, they maintain, about possessing weapons that one is not going to use.

These positions bristle with problems. 'Counter-force' nuclear warfare, for example, appears likely to be only the trigger of an inevitable process of escalation to total nuclear war. Furthermore, it seems self-delusionary to think oneself morally blameless in attacking military bases in the full knowledge that 25 million civilians will die of radiation sickness. Would it not be more honest simply to concede that, where nuclear weapons are concerned, one is always attacking civilians? And the Christian insight that what we plan in our hearts is as important as what we actually do (Matt. 5:28) would seem to apply with especial directness to nuclear weapons. For as the writings of military strategists have made clear, 'the real intention to use nuclear weapons, should the occasion arise, is an integral part of their deterrent nature.'[12]

Many Just War thinkers, however, have faced the moral challenge of nuclear weapons forthrightly and courageously. Their Christian commitment to justice, and to the principles of discrimination and proportion, has left them no other choice. Although in their realism they can still justify a 'lesser evil', they can realistically think of no evil that is greater than nuclear war. The lesser evil of our age, they maintain, is the risky route of renouncing nuclear weapons. Furthermore, although they can continue reluctantly to sanction Christian participation in discriminate warfare, they know that there is no

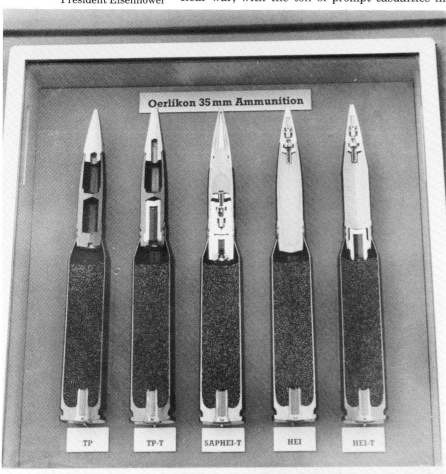

Oerlikon 35mm Ammunition

TP   TP-T   SAPHEI-T   HEI   HEI-T

way to have a nuclear war without killing millions of old people, women and children. This is the view of the committee of theologians and experts, chaired by the Bishop of Salisbury, which compiled *The Church and the Bomb*. This also is the conclusion of Evangelical spokesmen David Watson and John Stott.[13] John Stott, in an All Souls Langham Place Remembrance Day sermon in 1979, put it like this:

'[Because strategic nuclear weapons are] indiscriminate in their effects, destroying combatants and noncombatants alike, it seems clear to me that they are ethically indefensible, and that every Christian, whatever he may think of the possibility of a "just" use of conventional weapons, must be a nuclear pacifist.'[14]

'Every Christian must be a nuclear pacifist'. This is the message that is coming from the Just War tradition today. And its implications are immense. Just War Christians will have to think anew about the policies of the government; and their rethinking may cause them to depart from long-held political allegiances. They must also re-examine their jobs and be willing to abandon those positions that require them to do research into nuclear weapons, or to produce and handle them. This will lead some of them to become 'selective conscientious objectors' who reject, not all war, but unjust war. No more than the Germans of the Hitler era can Just Warriors participate in the preparation for holocaust. These steps will be costly. In an age of unemployment they will require that some of us give up our jobs. They will cause division and personal anguish. They will take us into uncharted territory. Being a nuclear pacifist will not be easy.

But as those who adhere to the Just War take the necessary steps of faithfulness, they will find that they have Christian allies, who also are working against nuclear weapons, but who have come to the same place via a different route. These are the pacifist Christians.

Questions for Study and Discussion

The Just War Doctrine

1. According to Alan Kreider, what conditions are necessary for a war to be called 'Just'?
2. '[Because strategic nuclear weapons are] in-

discriminate in their effects, destroying combatants and noncombatants alike, it seems clear to me that they are ethically indefensible, and that every Christian, whatever he may think of the possibility of a 'just' use of conventional weapons, must be a nuclear pacifist.'

Do you agree with this statement? Why, or why not?

Notes: The Just War Doctrine

1. For a historical study of the Just War, and of Christian pacifism, see Roland H. Bainton, *Christian Attitudes Toward War and Peace* (Abingdon Press, 1960).
2. An excellent brief presentation is that of Arthur Holmes, 'The Just War', in Robert G. Clouse, ed., *War: Four Christian Views* (InterVarsity Press [US], 1981), 117-135.
3. St. Augustine, *Letter 189* (to Boniface), in Augustine, *Works* (Nicene and Post-Nicene Fathers, 1st ser.), I.
4. John Eppstein, *The Catholic Tradition of the Law of Nations* (Catholic Association for International Peace, 1935), 57-61; Frederick H. Russel, *The Just War in the Middle Ages* (Cambridge University Press, 1975), 3-7, 16-39.
5. For a good summary of the biblical case for the Just War position, see Holmes, 'The Just War'. My own statement of the biblical argument for the Just War is lengthier than that of Holmes, and draws insight from a number of writers in addition to Holmes, particularly Paul Ramsey (*Basic Christian Ethics* [Charles Scribner's Sons, 1951], 166-184) and John Stott, 'The Biblical Argument: co-sponsored by the London Institute for Contemporary Christianity and the Shaftesbury Project for Nuclear Pacifism', address given at a conference, 16 October 1982 on 'The Christian Mind on the Arms Race'.
6. G. E. M. Anscombe, 'War and Murder', in Stein, *Nuclear Weapons and Christian Conscience* (Merlin, 1961), 53-54.
7. A. J. P. Taylor, *English History, 1914-1945* (Clarendon Press, 1965), 591n.
8. R. C. D. Jasper, *George Bell – Bishop of Chichester* (Oxford University Press, 1967), 276.
9. Cited by Sidney Lens, *The Day Before Doomsday: An Anatomy of the Nuclear Arms Race* (Doubleday, 1977), 251.
10. International Institute for Strategic Studies, *Strategic Survey 1981-1982* (IISS, 1982), 1.
11. Paul Ramsey, 'The Limits of Nuclear War', in Ramsey, *The Just War: Force and Political Responsibility* (Charles Scribner's Sons, 1968), 211-258.
12. Ruston, *Nuclear Deterrence*, 62.
13. David Watson, 'Jesus Christ Lives . . . so what, with the threat of nuclear holocaust?' (sermon at All Souls Langham Place, London, 9 May 1982; 'Interview with John Stott', *Cubit*, Autumn 1982, 5.
14. John Stott in *Christianity Today*, 8 February 1980.

Pacifist Christianity

Among Christians pacifism has an even longer history than does the Just War. In the three centuries closest to Jesus every Christian theologian who pronounced on the subject declared that believers must refuse to participate in warfare.[1] The early church's disciplinary regulations also maintained this position.[2] And even after the church's position began to diverge from this in the fourth century, a significant minority, in ordinary congregations as well as in renewal movements and religious orders, has continued to adhere to the church's original teachings.

Like the Just War, pacifism has not been a uniform position. Over the centuries Christian thinkers have formulated their pacifist convictions in many ways. One scholar, in fact, has recently discerned eighteen varieties of religious pacifism![3] I shall here be presenting, not a summary of all of these, but my own variety, which owes much to the thinking of others. With them I share the conviction that the justice which God wills cannot be attained by military means. Christians will therefore pursue justice and peace, not by taking life, but by beginning something new.

Undergirding pacifist Christianity are certain affirmations.

1. Because the world is marred by the Fall, Christians cannot escape from evil, which expresses itself in selfishness and greed and which leads to conflict. War is therefore an unavoidable part of human experience.

2. Through Jesus Christ, however, something new has begun. The Kingdom which he inaugurated can be entered only through conversion, for only in that way can we discover that a loving Father accepts us and cares for us. Since we therefore do not need to fear, we can respond freely to Jesus' teachings which turn upside-down our conventional assumptions about economic and physical security. Loving the enemy is simply one aspect of a comprehensive unconventional lifestyle which is rooted in a deep realisation that God is faithful. And the Kingdom, in which God's Holy Spirit is empowering men and women to respond in a new way to the 'unavoidabilities' of life, is literally a 'new creation'.

3. The church is the social expression of this newness. When it is faithful to its calling to be a reconciled family from tribes and nations which had formerly been enemies, and when it shares its possessions freely according to need, it is God's instrument for achieving peace and justice. Its corporate solidarity also enables its members to survive in a hostile and uncomprehending environment.

4. The forces of the Fall are terrified by newness. The experience of the participants in the 'new creation' will therefore be one of struggle as they come into conflict with 'lesser evils' such as war. In the struggle, they will only use means that are in keeping with the ends they seek. They will not dehumanise their opponents, inflict lasting harm on them, or place them beyond the possibility of repentance. In this conflict they will experience both suffering and the recreative power of God. The result of the struggle is certain, since Jesus, the Prince of Peace, on the cross has already defeated the Enemy.

Pacifism is thus not a romantic sentiment which wistfully desires the preservation of 'peace' at any price. It is a strenuously practical activity, in which men and women use unconventional means to combat evil. To describe the means which pacifists are called to use, we may imagine a spectrum of responses to evil. At the one extreme is utter inactivity (ignoring the evil); at the other extreme is blowing up the world (combatting the evil by committing, not only suicide, but cosmocide). Both the Just War and pacifism lie between these extremes. Adherents of the Just War and pacifism will combat evil with lethal violence, at times on a vast scale, so long as it

follows certain rules and thus remains a 'lesser evil'; they will not sanction blowing up women and children, to say nothing of the whole creation. Pacifists, on the other hand, will combat evil with methods that are not life-denying but are potentially life-giving. They are critical of those who remain passive for not taking evil seriously; they are equally critical of those who kill, even as a 'lesser evil', for not taking *their own evil* seriously enough.

In the area between inactivity and killing, there are many means of struggle: praying for the enemy, debating, engaging in political activity, demonstrating, restraining the mugger, conversing with the enemy, engaging in non-cooperation and civil disobedience. None of these means will inflict lasting damage on the enemy; none of these will dehumanise him or deny him the chance to explain his position; none of them is in conflict with the desired end of a just peace. But all of these means are costly, and can lead to the suffering and death, not of the enemy, but of oneself; all of them, by valuing the enemy's person, can lead to his repentance and reconciliation; all of them, by entering uncharted territory in which known precedents are few, compel us in our vulnerability to trust God, who is our security. And they offer exciting possibilities. Who can tell what will happen if a believer lovingly disobeys the order of a dehumanised person? Perhaps his disobedience will sow the seeds of the person's discovery of what it means to be a child of God! But these forms of struggle should not be evaluated by their effectiveness in achieving some end. If they are loving and peaceable, they reflect the character of God and thus have value enough in themselves. As A. J. Muste put it, 'There is no way to peace. Peace is the way!'

Pacifism is thus not passivism; it is active peacemaking in combat with evil. But to many people pacifism *sounds* passive; it has overtones of self-righteousness and unconcern about justice. For this reason, many people have hunted for a better label for this position. 'Non-violent activism' is the most common of these. 'Aggressive vulnerability' (Faith Lees) is in many ways a more perceptive alternative.[4] I myself have a special affection for 'the violence of pacifists', with which Brother Roger Schutz of Taizé has attempted to emphasise that true peacemaking must grow out of struggle.[5] But despite *pacifism's* sleepy connotations, I continue to use the word.

Its Latin roots (*pax* [peace] – *facio* [make]) mean peacemaking. And that after all is the point, for peacemakers are what the sons and daughters of God are called to be (Matt. 5:9). As James put it (Jas. 3:18), 'the harvest of justice is sown in peace by peacemakers'.

Pacifism, unlike the Just War, has no genetic connection with pagan philosophers in the natural law tradition. Its origins are exclusively Biblical, preeminently in the person and work of Jesus of Nazareth. And its approach collapses if God is not a loving Father who protects his children and provides for them, and if Jesus is not Messsiah and Lord. A position that is validated by the resurrection collapses if resurrection doesn't happen! But although pacifist Christians find their position fully stated for the first time in the New Testament, they can also trace its roots in the *Old Testament*.[6] For in both testaments, they agree with adherents of the Just War, God reveals himself as a God of love whose will is justice and peace.

1. *War is the result of the Fall*. The first recorded interpersonal sin was murder (Gen. 4:8-9). And although God protected the murderer Cain from retribution, soon Lamech was engaging in massive vengeance (Gen. 4:1-5; 22-23). Men made weapons and the earth was full of violence (Gen. 4:22; 6:11,13). God therefore destroyed the human race by flood, except for a remnant based on Noah's descendants with whom he began anew.

2. *Election of a representative people*. Through Abraham, who left the security of his home in response to his call, God began to form a people who would be his instruments in reversing the effects of the Fall. Having a covenant relationship with himself, they would be both *like himself* ('Be holy [set apart], for I am holy' [Lev. 11:44]) and *unlike other nations* ('You shall not walk in the customs of the nations' [Lev. 20:23]). Through them, in the fullness of time, God would bring his blessing to all nations (Gen. 12:4). Abraham and his children were primarily pacifistic in their dealings with their rivals (Gen. 13:26; cf. Gen. 14). To find food in a time of dearth, Jacob and his clan took refuge in Egypt, where after several generations they, as unwanted aliens, became slave labourers. God heard their cry under oppression.

God formed his people into a nation by liberating them miraculously from slavery. After a crescendo of miracles which compelled Pharaoh to let the Israelites leave Egypt, God defeated the Egyptian military machine in the battle of the Red Sea. He did so by nature-miracle, and the Israelites had only to 'be still' (Exo. 14). God thereby established that liberation was his gift of grace, and not the result of the Israelites' works or prowess. As their King, he miraculously provided his people with both food and protection.

3. *Holy War (by miracle)*. In the 'Holy War' God as Israel's King continued the distinctive form of fighting which he had used in the Exodus. Although the Israelites might fight in a secondary capacity (and at times with genocidal violence), the victor was God whose means was miracle.[7] A crumbling wall, a swollen stream, a rumour, a hornet, thunder, a loud sound – all of these were God's means of defeating Israel's foes, and not, he reminded them, 'your sword or your bow' (Josh. 24:12). To make sure that his people would depend upon his protection, God decreed that the Israelites should be both numerically and technologically weaker than their enemies (Deut. 20:1-9; Josh. 11:6,9). He was especially concerned that they not acquire *chariots,* the capital military weapons of that era which most of their enemies possessed. For he wanted his children to be a distinctive ('holy') nation, in their unmilitarised dependence upon himself.

4. *Pagan imitation*. Despite his miraculous protection, Israel rejected God as their King. Instead they chose a human 'king *like all the nations* ... [who will] go out before us and fight our battles' (1 Sam. 8:20). Grieved at this, the Lord warned the Israelites that their rejection of him as their protector and provider would lead to militarism and materialism, as a result of which they would be their king's slaves (1 Sam. 8:11-18). Shortly thereafter Israel began to acquire chariots (2 Sam. 8:4) and to develop a social hierarchy of rich and very poor whose apex was in the royal court. Israel had become a typical ancient Near Eastern society.

5. *Prophetic protest*. Prophets thereupon arose to speak God's word to his militaristic children. The prophets appealed to Israel's history, not to urge a policy based on military strength, but rather to call the people to repentance, trusting in God rather than weapons (Isa. 31:1 ff.; Jer. 32:20 ff.; Hos. 13:4 ff.). When they did repent, God still performed acts of miraculous deliverance (2 Kings 18-19; 2 Chron. 20:32; Isa. 37; cf. 2 Kings 6:11 ff.). But when they persisted in trusting in weapons and oppressing the poor, God used war to judge their militarism and materialism (Isa. 2:7 ff.) 'Trust in chariots' led to the 'tumult of war' (Hos. 10:13-14). Security forces led to insecurity: 'The nations have sunk in the pit which they made; in the net which they hid has their own foot been caught' (Ps. 9:15). Because of their militaristic infidelity, God, who had fought for his people, was now fighting against them: 'Behold I am against you, and I will burn your chariots in smoke' (Nah. 2:13). The inevitable result was defeat, humiliation, exile and occupation.

6. *Prophetic promise*. The prophets also foretold the coming of a day when God would do a 'new thing'. Then he would write his 'new covenant' on his people's hearts and pour out his Spirit on all flesh (Jer. 31:31 ff.; Joel 2:28-29). His means would be a perfect King, an Anointed One, who would establish justice by meek means, ride on a donkey instead of a charger, and 'cut off the chariot from Ephraim' (Zech. 9:9-10). The King would be a Servant who through his own suffering would give healing, forgiveness and life (Isa. 53). Through him God would reconstitute his people, combining a faithful remnant of the Jewish people with men and women drawn from every nation. Once again a holy nation, they would manifest their distinctive qualities by 'beating their swords into ploughshares and their spears into pruninghooks' (Isa. 2:2-4; 10:20-22; Micah 4:1-3).

The Old Testament materials which we have just surveyed have often embarrassed pacifists. Some of them, talking of their 'New Testament faith', have heretically divided Scripture and conceded the Old Testament to the adherents of the Just War. They have done so for understandable reasons, for some Old Testament passages – such as those in which God commanded his children to engage in genocide – are hard for pacifists to stomach. But then the Old Testament is no easier for non-pacifist Christians to cope with. Adherents of the Just War find genocide (the mass slaying of noncombatants as well as combatants) to be ethically incomprehensible. And no modern Christian soldier really wants to take the Old Testament seriously when it commands God's people to be numerically and technologically inferior to their foes.

On the other hand, a careful reading of both Testaments show their fundamental unity.[8] In

'...and they shall beat their swords into ploughshares.'

the 'new covenant' God fulfills the 'old covenant'; in it he brings his unfolding revelation to its culmination in the Messiah Jesus, who is his final and perfect word about himself (Heb. 1:1), and whose teaching reveals the intention behind the Old Testament Law. It is through the Messiah that the disciples expectantly read the earlier Scriptures (Luke 24:25-27). And when we do so, we not surprisingly find in both Testaments the same God – who is gracious and longsuffering; who is forming a people to do his will and to demonstrate his purposes to all nations; who liberates his people from oppression, protects us and provides for us; who is jealous of our worship and dependance; and whose will, which will not be frustrated, is justice and peace for the whole creation.

In the *New Testament* the hope and expectation of the Old Testament prophets were fulfilled in Jesus, the Messiah of Israel and the Son of God.

1. *The historical setting.* The Palestine into which Jesus was born was an oppressed country. Indeed, because it was ruled by a Roman colonial government which was politically and economically exploiting the Jewish people and offending their religious convictions, it was a 'politico-religious tinderbox'.[9] One Jewish party, the Zealots, had become an active force of religious revolutionaries which was organising to expel the Romans by military means. When Jesus was a boy, the Romans had put down a Zealot uprising by crucifying two thousand people on the hills outside of Nazareth.[10] In this tense and expectant setting, the Jewish people would view any potential Messiah-king as either a Zealot or as a collaborator. From the start of his ministry, Jesus was therefore compelled to deal with issues of liberation, justice and violence.

2. *The coming of Jesus.* Into this violent and oppressive situation God sent his Son Jesus. After being anointed in God's Spirit as Messiah, Jesus began to proclaim the dawning of a new age, the manifestation of God's kingly reign on earth (Mark 1:14 ff.). In himself and his mission, Jesus declared, what the prophets and righteous ones of old had longed to see was now being fulfilled (Matt. 13:17).

a. *Kingdom of God.* Jesus not only proclaimed the Kingdom of God; he embodied it and brought it. For it was in Jesus himself, in his person and deeds, that God was at work healing the sick,

feeding the hungry, freeing the oppressed and binding up the broken-hearted (Luke 4:16-21). As well as being the perfect demonstration of God's character and concerns, Jesus was also the instrument of the Father's rule. He took authority over illness and oppression; and he resolutely embraced outsiders and the victims of injustice (the poor, women, Samaritans, tax-collectors). At exploitation, especially in the name of religion, he became angry. In a non-violent demonstration (he used his whip only against animals) he cleansed the Temple, reclaiming for outsiders the precinct (the Court of the Gentiles) which had been turned into a market for Jews (John 2:13 ff.).[11] In all his dealings he was both regal and humble. Always the 'suffering servant', he dramatised his life's mission by washing his disciples' feet (John 13:1-16).

b. *Repentance and faith.* God's work in Jesus required men and women to respond by repenting and believing (Mark 1:15). Only by being converted and becoming like little children could they enter the Kingdom of God (Matt. 18:4). And this meant that they must see with new eyes, leave behind 'normal' sources of security, and trust wholly in God's Fatherly reign (Matt. 7:7-11). Because of their conversion, the children of the Kingdom were bound to have social values that were unconventional.[12] Here, in the new age, it is the dependent (the poor, the powerless servants) who are great, not the self-sufficient (the rich, the powerful benefactors). The children of the Kingdom, among whom God is constructing a new society, will thus be different from the dominant figures of the old age. Having freed them from fear and insecurity, God is empowering them to live an alternative lifestyle based on trust.

c. *Discipleship.* To those who were drawn to him in conversion and faith, Jesus responded with an invitation and command: 'Follow me!' Be my disciples; learn from me. Master my teachings; imitate me as your model. Thereby you will experience and express the new social order which God has begun in me.

3. *The teachings of Jesus.*

a. *God is Father.* At the heart of Jesus' proclamation was his assertion that God is Father. No longer the distant deity who must be placated by observance of ritual or law, God emerged in Jesus' teaching as *Abba*, Daddy, the pursuing forgiver, whom his children can know intimately

'Any act of war aimed indiscriminately at entire cities or extensive areas along with their population is a crime against God and man himself. It merits unequivocal and unhesitating condemnation.'

Vatican II

(Luke 15:11 ff.). The Father is lovingly aware of his creation; he knows his children's needs; he cares for their protection and provision. Therefore his children, unlike the pagans, do not need to be anxious (Matt. 6:25-33). No longer do they need to clutch their plans, possessions, or self-protective devices. 'Do not be afraid, little flock, for the Father has chosen to give you the Kingdom' (Luke 12:32).

b. *Love your enemies*. Jesus' teachings on violence are expressions of God's Fatherhood and Kingdom. They are not the sage words of a great teacher; nor are they good advice about how to get one's way without suffering. They, like Jesus' teachings on possessions, are expressions of his profound trust in a gracious and powerful Father who protects his children and provides for them.

These teachings grew out of Jesus' constant confrontation with violence as a genuine option. In Roman Palestine, violence was in the air; as Messiah-king he encountered the military option repeatedly, from his temptations in the wilderness to his agonising testing in Gethsemane. It is therefore not surprising that Jesus was utterly realistic in his assessment of violence. He observed accurately that violence breeds violence ('They that take the sword perish by it' [Matt. 26:52]); and he knew that bearers of his message would encounter violent opposition both within families and from political and religious leaders (Matt. 10:34-36; Luke 12:51-53). When he was informed that King Herod was plotting to kill him, he was not in the least shocked (Luke 13:31-32).[13]

An indication of the importance of this issue to Jesus is the fact that in the gospel of Luke *he devoted his very first ethical teaching to military violence*. 'Love your enemies', he commanded his disciples (Luke 6:27). Likewise in the Sermon on the Mount, in which he established a 'pattern of life in the Kingdom of God', three of the six antitheses have to do with violence, culminating once again with 'Love your enemies' (Matt. 5:21-48).

But what did Jesus mean? Since the fourth century, scholars have attempted in numerous ways to demonstrate that Jesus was not telling his disciples to refrain from killing in time of war. Several of these are:

1) *Personal ethic*. Jesus had personal enemies in mind, not national enemies. I am to love the individual who persecutes me, or who steals my notebook on the eve of an exam, but not the Romans/Russians.

2) *Ethics of intention (attitude)*. Jesus had national enemies in mind, but his true concern had to do not with actions but with attitudes. When I, at the order of my government, reluctantly kill Romans/Russians, in my heart I must cherish love for them.

3) *Ad interim ethic*. Jesus had national enemies in mind. But he intended this and other strenuous aspects of his teaching to apply only until the end of the world, which he thought was imminent. Jesus was wrong. Therefore I along with other Christians must be more realistic in the way I order my life, and if necessary must kill Romans/Russians.

4) *Post interim ethic* (dispensationalism). Jesus had national enemies in mind. But the church rejected his teachings, so that they will not come fully into force until he returns in the Millenium. Until then in wartime I must kill Romans/Russians.

5) *Ethic of counsels and precepts* (some Roman Catholics). Jesus had national enemies in mind. But his teaching in this case (as in relinquishing possessions and celibacy) applies only to those who, by obeying the 'evangelical counsels', are seeking to be perfect (Matt. 5:48). Since the cohesion of society requires that ordinary believers behave more normally in response to biblical teachings which clearly apply to everyone ('precepts'), they will in wartime kill Romans/Russians, while those with a special (generally priestly) vocation will abstain.

Any of these alternative interpretations could of course be correct, and Jesus would be speaking in more common-sense language if they were. But all of them, I am convinced, are wrong. Jesus expected his disciples to find his teachings difficult ('I say *to you that can hear me,* Love your enemies' [Luke 6:27]). But he expected them to obey him. It was those who 'hear these words of mine and do them' who are building their house on the rock (Matt. 7:24). And although throughout the Sermon on the Mount Jesus showed tremendous psychological insight about attitudes, nowhere, neither in the case of lust nor of enemy-hatred, does he justify actions that are incompatible with inner attitudes. In his first epistle, John rightly expressed Jesus' meaning: 'Love must be genuine, and show itself in action' (1 Jn. 3:18 NEB). Nor is there any indication that these teachings are only for an elite nucleus of

disciples. All of Jesus' followers are called to be perfect, complete, merciful, mature, and thus to reflect the character of the Father (Matt. 5:48; Luke 6:36; cf. Eph. 4:13 and Col. 1:28), in which believers are enjoined to be *mature* [the same Greek word as *perfect*] in Christ.

But was Jesus telling his disciples to love their *national* enemies? Certainly it was hard enough for them to love their personal competitors. True. Loving personal enemies could not have been easy, and Jesus gave them instructions about loving persecutors, those who cursed and abused them, even those who struck them on the face (Matt. 5:44; Luke 6:28-29).

But did Jesus have national enemies in mind as well, perhaps especially national enemies? Of course he did. For one thing, when the word 'enemies' is used in the Gospels it generally means national enemies. In Luke 1:71, 74-75 the 'enemies' were those who hated the Jewish people and who were preventing them from serving God in holiness and justice without fear. The Romans, clearly. In Luke 19:43-44 the 'enemies' once again were doing deeds of a markedly military character – erecting siege engines against Jerusalem, destroying the city and killing its people. Again the Romans. When we recall the setting in which Jesus was teaching, this will be understandable. Palestine was an occupied country. Cells of Zealot guerillas were active in it. In such a setting, it would have been surprising if a Rabbi who had begun his teaching by saying 'Love your enemies' had *not* meant the Roman oppressors. This hardly makes Jesus' teaching easier to take, but in his situation it at least enables him to make sense.

Jesus notably did not tell his disciples to love their enemies because it is a good technique and gets results; he did not tell them to love the Romans so that they obligingly would leave Galilee for the Galileans. Jesus' reasons were rather twofold. If you love your enemies, Jesus told them, *you will be different*. You will be different from the tax-collectors, who collaborated with the Romans, and from the Romans (Gentiles) themselves, both of whom love only their own kind (Matt. 5:46-47). 'You don't want to be like your oppressors, do you?' one can hear Jesus asking his disciples. On the contrary, if you love your enemies, *you will be like your Father* (Matt. 5:45, 48). The Father, who frees his children from fear, thereby frees them to love, even their enemies.

'Sons of the Father' not only have a relationship of Abba-intimacy with the Father; they also bear the family likeness, reflect his character and act like he does. And, says Jesus, it is peacemakers and enemy-lovers who are the Father's children (Matt. 5:9, 44-45). For the Father's purpose is to incorporate men and women from *all nations* into his people. He sends his rain on the unjust as well as the just; he loves *his* enemies (cf. Rom. 5:8-10). Be like Abba! Be merciful, as your Father is merciful. Be complete, as he is complete (Matt. 5:45, 48; Luke 6:36).

So Jesus proceeded to gather disciples who would be 'sons of peace' (Luke 10:5-9). They would be involved in struggle for the Kingdom. But in order to be struggling as the Father's children for *his* Kingdom, they must go *beyond retaliation*. The Law, limiting the massive retribution of primitive society (Gen. 4:24) to retaliation in kind, had said, 'An eye for an eye and a tooth for a tooth' (Exo. 21:24; Matt. 5:38 ff.). Jesus, in the knowledge that the Father's intention is not to limit but end retaliation, tells his disciples, 'Do not resist one who is evil' (Matt. 5:39). Some Christians have used this verse to construct a doctrine of absolute non-resistance; others have used it as a pretext to dismiss Jesus' teaching as unrealistic or exaggerated. But it is unlikely that Jesus, whose whole life was a resistance to evil, was telling his disciples not to do what he himself was doing. His teaching here rather must be understood as a statement of another aspect of his positive command to love the enemy.[14] Thus what Jesus is saying here is, 'Do not resist the evil ones by their means'. As Paul interpreted this text, 'Do not be overcome by evil, but overcome evil with good' (Rom. 12:21; 1 Thess. 5:15). Or Peter: 'Do not return evil for evil, or reviling for reviling; but on the contrary bless, for to this you have been called' (1 Pet. 3:9). By doing good to their antagonists, by blessing those who curse them, by interceding before the Father for their persecutors, the disciples may be opening the way to the conversion of their enemies, setting them in a new relationship to God and other people.

4. *The rejection of Jesus.* The Jewish people and their leaders rejected his teaching. The Jerusalem crowds acclaimed him; but Jesus grieved over the city because it 'did not know the things that make for peace' (Luke 19:41-42). Accurately he anticipated the destruction which the Romans would impose upon the city for its militaristic

tendencies which culminated in the rebellion of A.D. 66-70. Within five days the crowds had turned against the enemy-loving Jesus and were calling for him to be crucified. In his place, they chose Barabbas, a Zealot who had committed murder in an insurrection, whose attitude to the Romans they could understand (Luke 23:19). The Jewish authorities, on the other hand, had all along found Jesus to be threatening. His searching criticisms of the Temple-cult and of their piety had struck home. Furthermore, they were afraid of how the Romans might respond to him. So the authorities engaged in a pragmatic, 'lesser evil' calculation. To safeguard the national interest ('it is expedient that one man should die for the people, and that the whole nation should not perish' [Jn. 11:50]), they proceeded to engineer Jesus' crucifixion.

5. *The Cross.* The Jewish and Roman leaders in Palestine represented the highest achievements of ancient civilisation – Jewish faith and Roman government. But in their fear and pride they did not recognise, in Jesus' almighty meekness, the 'Lord of glory'. To protect themselves from the criticism of his words and example, they therefore collaborated to crucify him (1 Cor. 2:8). By accepting their unjust sentence, Jesus not only demonstrated the nature of true authority; he also exposed the hollowness of their pretensions. Showing Jewish piety to be faithless and Roman justice to be unjust, he 'disarmed the principalities and powers' (Col. 2:15). At the climax of history Jesus thus performed the ultimate act of disarmament.[15]

Crucifixion was the most brutal form of execution known to the ancient world. As Jesus submitted to it, all of the violence, hatred and sin of the human race was focused upon him. As curses were being flung at him, he was becoming a curse for us, so that God's blessing of Abraham might extend to the whole human family, including the enemy Gentiles who were killing him (Deut. 21:23; Gal. 3:13-14). By accepting his alienation from God and all people, Jesus was opening to all the possibility of fellowship with their Father and their estranged sisters and brothers. Dying as he lived, to the end Jesus was a 'suffering servant'. And thereby, as he bore the punishment for our iniquities, he was ratifying a 'new covenant' in his blood (Isa. 53; 1 Cor. 11:28; Heb. 8-10).

6. *Resurrection and the Holy Spirit.* On the third day, by miracle, God demonstrated that his Kingdom would not be frustrated by human violence. He raised Jesus from the grave. Thereby he not only vindicated his Son's suffering servanthood; he also destroyed Satan's power, which had been based on the unanswerable sanction of the 'final solution' – death. By coming through death, Jesus became the pioneer who, going on in advance of his brothers and sisters, has freed us 'who through fear of death were subject to lifelong bondage' to sinful appetites and institutions (Heb. 2:5-15). By overcoming death and fear, he has reversed the Fall and inaugurated the 'new creation' in which we can begin to live freely in a new way. After having taught his followers about the Kingdom of God, the resurrected Jesus ascended, joining the Father in reigning lordship (Acts 1:1-11). On Pentecost he then came back to his followers through the Holy Spirit, who has actualised his presence and power among us. In the Spirit he has anointed us, freeing us from the fearful spirit of slavery, and giving us the liberating Spirit of sonship in whom we know God as Abba (Rom. 8:12-22).

7. *A new society.* The Spirit is shaping reborn men and women into a new corporate reality, the Church. As the people of God under the new covenant, it is both smaller than any nation yet also vastly greater than any nation. In it *reconciliation* is taking place.[16] Men and women from groups who had been enemies – slave, free, male, female, Jew, Gentile, even the 'barbarians' who are commonly viewed as a threat to established values – are finding their peace in the Messiah (Gal. 3:28; Col. 2:11). In him, the members of the new 'Israel of God' (Gal. 6:16) have found a new primary identity: Christian. These reconciled enemies cannot take life in war. For they recognise that their nation's enemies of the moment are either present or potential brothers and sisters.

The people of God are one in the Messiah. They are the continuation of his earthly life; and since they embody his presence they live unconventionally in obedience to his commandments (Jn. 14:23). As 'the body of Christ', its members' concerns are the same as those of Jesus during his lifetime. The members will heal the sick, free the oppressed, and bind up the brokenhearted. They will make peace in situations of conflict, strive for justice for the poor and the outsiders, and share their possessions with each other and with the weak (Jas. 3:18; 2 Cor. 8; 1

John 3:17). The gospel to which they bear witness is the 'gospel of peace' (Acts 10:36). Together, as they assist each other to be obedient to Jesus' teachings which as individuals they find daunting, they are experiencing the 'new creation' and bringing in the justice and peace of the Kingdom of God (Gal. 6:15).

8. *Nonconformity and struggle.* The body of Christ is no more at peace with the forces of the Fall than Jesus himself had been (John 15:20). Like him it is involved in a struggle with principalities, powers, and 'world rulers of this present darkness' (Eph. 6:12 ff.). At times these spiritual/political forces are faithful to their divinely-assigned task of promoting the good. When their stewardship of their authority is thus in keeping with God's Kingdom, Jesus' disciples will be subordinate (Rom. 13:1-7; 1 Peter 2:13-14). But when they are oppressing the good, flaunting their pomp and amassing instruments of violence, the disciples will respond with prophetic but respectful disobedience (Acts 5:29; Rev. 13:4-10). For the disciples recognise only one real authority in the world – that of God as revealed in the executed Galilean carpenter who has disarmed the powers. The disciples therefore know that there are not two standards of behaviour – one for individual Christians and the other for governments. There is one standard, that of Jesus who is Lord of all.[17] And he calls his followers, not to domination and vengeance, but to prophetic witness to *his* rule and to love – of both brothers/sisters and enemies (Rom. 12:10, 14, 17-21). These are acts of social nonconformity (Rom. 12:2); they will be misintepreted and feared, leading to persecution for the disciples (2 Tim. 3:12). Like Jesus the disciples will be suffering servants, bearing their crosses in which forgiveness absorbs hostility (1 Peter 2:21-24; Luke 14:27; Eph. 4:32-5:2).

9. *Final things.* Ours are the 'last days' in which there will be 'wars and rumours of war' (Acts 2:17; Matt. 24:6). As history approaches its climax of judgement, there will be conflagrations which will terrify 'the kings of the earth and the great men and the generals and the rich and strong and every one' (Rev. 6:15). Throughout these catastrophes, Jesus' followers will remain constant. Nowhere does the Bible call them to apocalyptic violence. It rather calls them to faithfulness in their proper callings of prayer, patient endurance and faith (Rev. 1:9; 2:19; 6:9-11;

13:10). With their words and lives they are to bear witness (martyrdom). 'Jesus is Lord!' God's Kingdom is 'justice, peace and joy in the Holy Spirit' (Rom. 14:17). Expectantly the disciples will live, working for these qualities which will surely triumph, and awaiting the Day when God will wipe away all tears and 'make all things new' (Rev. 21:1-5). This then is a case for pacifist Christianity. Like the Just War doctrine, it is a serious attempt to understand Scripture. And like the Just War doctrine, it is concerned to limit violence.

But differences between pacifism and the Just War doctrine are as striking as the similarities. I shall not list these here. By now many will be apparent to you. But one basic difference between the two approaches, to which Miss Anscombe has already referred (see quote on p.00 above), is worth discussing briefly. Miss Anscombe contrasts the 'practicable' characteristics of the Just War doctrine with the 'beautifully ideal but impracticable' characteristics of pacifism; for her, it is a matter of realism versus idealism. As a pacifist Christian, I would rather state the comparison otherwise; for me, the difference is between accepting the world as it is and seeking to change it. Whereas the adherents of the Just War view the fallen state of the world as largely unalterable but controllable in some of its nastier aspects, the pacifist Christian senses a call to participate in a new world which God is building, and to invite the old world to join in.

To get into the new world, one must begin to see things differently. 'The penny must drop.' One must get a glimpse of the Kingdom of God and think that it might actually be coming. There must then be a far-reaching and painful restructuring of one's assumptions and lifestyle according to Jesus' 'upside-down' standards. For Jesus' 'hard sayings' cannot be taken piecemeal; they all fit together. And they not only apply to violence (Unfortunately, many pacifists are strict interpreters solely of Jesus' teachings on violence!); they also lead to radical approaches to other areas of life, such as leadership and material possessions. The comprehensiveness of conversion, which freed the early Christians from the various forms of bondage of their former life, was well expressed by Justin Martyr, who in 165 A.D. was beheaded in Rome:

'Those who once rejoiced in fornication now delight in continence alone; those who made use of magic arts have dedicated themselves to the good and unbegotten God; we who once took most pleasure in the means of increasing our wealth and property now bring what we have into a common fund and share with everyone in need; we who hated and killed one another and would not associate with men of different tribes because of their different customs, now after the manifestation of Christ live together and pray for our enemies and try to persuade those who unjustly hate us, so that they, living according to the fair commands of Christ, may share with us the good hope of receiving the same things ... [Christ's] sayings were short and concise, for he was no sophist, but his word was the power of God.'

(Justin, I Apology, 14).

Of course, to live like this is to flout the accepted wisdom of self-preservation. Without material and military strength, one in one's helplessness is forced to depend upon God for provision and protection. The consequences of this are unknowable. But to pacifist Christians consequences are of secondary importance. What matters is Christ's 'short and concise' sayings, undergirded by the Father's reliable love. Or to put it like Paul did, 'the only thing that counts is new creation' (Gal. 6:15 NEB).

If faithfulness to Christ's teachings brings suffering and the cross, that is only what he promised us, along with his all-sufficient grace (2 Cor. 12:9). On the other hand, pacifist Christians are convinced that God still does work miracles of provision and protection; and, lest they 'forget all his benefits', they have collected stories of incidents in which he has vindicated his people's unworldly-wise fidelity.[18] Antagonists have behaved inexplicably; new methods of 'non-violent resistance' have been fruitful; enemies have been reconciled.

What pacifists will be called to do in specific circumstances can thus not be predicted. The rules governing their action are less detailed than those of the Just War doctrine; guiding their behaviour is a simple positive command ('Love your enemy!') with its corresponding negative command ('Do not kill'), applied by prayer and the discernment of their communities of faith. These commands will make it impossible for pacifists to hold certain jobs. They will find it impossible to work in the armed forces, in defence-re-

lated industries and research, and in the military branches of the civil service. They will likewise not be able to hold political office that might require them to order the taking of life. A pacifist could not, at this point in English history, be Prime Minister! Although in many societies pacifists would not be able to serve as policemen, in the UK, whose police force is largely unarmed, this may be an appropriate avenue of Christian service. But pacifists should be reluctant to tell others what to do. After bearing witness to their understanding of Scripture, they should leave the application of their witness to the Spirit's work in the other's conscience. As the early Quaker George Fox told the newly-converted gentleman William Penn, who had asked whether he must stop wearing his sword, 'Wear it as long as you are able!'

The main concern of pacifist Christians, however, must not be avoiding 'no-go-areas'; it must be finding areas in which they can be *peacemakers,* doing positive and distinctive things which will bring in the newness of God's Kingdom. Since these will often be new ventures, on the fringes of society, they are hard to categorise. An old age pensioner goes to live in Derry, where both Protestant and Catholic paramilitaries discover that he, in his defencelessness, can be a trusted intermediary. A history student decides to do research into the largely unchronicled story of non-violent social change. A theology student, fired by his gospel vision of reconciliation, decides to establish a Christian conflict resolution service. A scientist – aware that 90 per cent of the research scientists in world history are living today and that at least half of them are working on military projects – decides to do research into the 'transarmament' by which 'defence industries' can be converted to civilian production. These and other similar actions will be poorly funded, precarious and suspect. But they will contain the seeds of newness.

There are, however, three major areas in which pacifist Christians will have a distinctive contribution to make. The first and most basic of these is the calling *to participate in 'God's new society',* the Church. God's chosen means of conveying his wisdom to the principalities and powers is that of Christian faith-communities (Eph. 3:10). In their common life, justice and reconciliation will be evidences of the presence of God's reign. Pacifist Christians will thus commit themselves deeply to make their churches into communities of *shalom.* The world may be falling apart, and there may be political activities that are ever so urgent; but for Christians there can be no short-cut to world peace that bypasses the Church. It is a matter of credibility; it is a matter of witness. If Christ is not Prince of Peace in the family of faith, how can there be witness to his reign elsewhere?

A second important calling to pacifist Christians is *to be prophetic.* Since this is a calling which Just War and pacifist Christians share, I shall discuss it in my final section dealing with common affirmations. But there is one prophetic responsibility which is unique to pacifists. This is querying the *myth of realism.* For centuries pacifists have been told that their ideas are 'impracticable'. What then is practicable? Pacifists must remind the world that it is 'realistic' thinking in economic and military matters (including that of adherents of the Just War) that has led the world to its current position of peril under the mushroom cloud. It may be 'realistic', but it is not reasonable, to expect peace when some people are rich and others are impoverished. It may be 'realistic', but it is not reasonable, to expect anything other than conflagration to come from an arms race. Sometimes – perhaps all along – the more realistic thing to do is something 'unrealistic'.

The third calling to pacifist Christians is *to engage in political action.* Pacifists will not do so because they believe that the world's problems are primarily political. Nor will they do so in an attempt to persuade governments to adopt pacifist policies. Christian pacifists must remember that their convictions are rooted in the very heart of their faith (God as Father, Jesus as 'suffering servant' and resurrected Lord) and are backed up by their willingness to follow Christ in suffering. They cannot expect this of their fellow citizens who are not believers. But they also know that justice and peace are God's will for the world, and that they are ultimately in everyone's interest. Therefore pacifists will try to persuade governments to be *more just and less violent* than they think is possible.[19]

Pacifists will especially try to influence national thinking and government policy in three areas in which they can make specifically Christian contributions to peacemaking. In foreign policy, they will have a special concern for reconciliation between 'irreconcilable' enemies. Pacifists were on the forefront of efforts to break down barriers between two nations which had been enemies for a millenium – France and Germany. They should be similarly active today in building relationships with Russians and East Germans. In military policy, pacifists will work to encourage the consideration of less violent and non-violent strategies in both policing and national defence. And in the areas of weaponry, pacifists will do everything they can, by means both orthodox and unorthodox (including voting, organising, lobbying, and demonstrating), to persuade the nation to 'turn its heart' about the nuclear weapons which are threatening millions of its and its enemy's people with a 'sudden end' (Zeph. 1:18).

This, of course, will bring the pacifist Christians into close collaboration with Christians of another ethical tradition who share their moral revulsion at nuclear weapons – the adherents of the Just War. 'We do not perceive any situation in which the deliberate initiation of nuclear warfare, on however restricted a scale, can be morally justified'.[20] This statement, in the draft pastoral letter (1982) to US Roman Catholics from the US National Conference of Bishops, is a platform on which Just Warriors and pacifists can stand together.

Questions for Study and Discussion

Pacifist Christianity

1. What is the biblical basis for the pacifist position?
2. Jesus' followers are to be like little children, 'leaving behind normal sources of security and trusting wholly in God's fatherly reign' (p.-). What, for you are 'normal' sources of security? What would it mean to leave these behind and trust wholly in God?
3. 'The Father who frees his children from fear, thereby frees them to love, even their enemies' (p.00). What are we afraid of? What fears keep us from being free to express Christ's love?
4. 'Pacifists will combat evil with methods that are not life-denying but are potentially life-giving' (p.00). What does this mean to you? How do you deny life to others – put others down, de-humanise them? What are possible life-giving ways of combating evil?
5. Jesus told his followers that by loving their enemies 1. *They would be different* and 2. *They would be like their Father*. Do we 'reflect the family likeness' or are we reflecting the fears and fantasies, the spirit and ideas of our age?
6. What areas can you find in which to be a peace-maker? As an individual? As a group? At home, at work, at church?

Notes: Pacifist Christianity

1. Roland H. Bainton, 'The Early Church and War', *Harvard Theological Review*, 39 (1946), 197; and the standard modern treatment, Jean-Michel Hornus, *It is Not Lawful for Me to Fight: Early Christian Attitudes toward War* (Herald Press, 1980).
2. Hippolytus, *Apostolic Tradition*, ch. 16, in G. J. Cuming, ed., *Hippolytus: A Text for Students* (Grove Booklets, 1976), 16; Hornus, *It is Not Lawful*, 162-173.
3. John H. Yoder, *Nevertheless: The Varieties of Religious Pacifism* (Herald Press, 1971).
4. Faith Lees, *Break Open My World: Personal Renewal Today* (Marshall Morgan & Scott, 1982), 38.
5. Dom Helder Camara, *The Conversions of a Bishop* (Collins, 1979), 179.
6. Millard C. Lind, *Yahweh is a Warrior: The Theology of Warfare in Ancient Israel* (Herald Press, 1980); Vernard Eller, *War and Peace from Genesis to Revelation* (Herald Press, 1981), ch. 1-4.
7. For perceptive comments on the theological rationale for the genocidal character of the 'Holy War' (*herem*), see John H. Yoder, 'If Abraham is Our Father', in his *The Original Revolution* (Herald Press, 1972), 104-105.
8. For helpful insights on the relationship between the Testaments with reference to the problem of war, see Willard M. Swartley, *Case Issues in Biblical Interpretation: Slavery, Sabbath, War and Women* (Herald Press, 1983), ch. 3.
9. Martin Hengel, *Victory over Violence* (SPCK Press, 1975), 56.
10. Josephus, *Antiquities of the Jews*, XVII, x, 5, 10, in his *Complete Works*, trans. William Whiston (Pickering and Inglis, 1960), 371-372.
11. Recent translations (NIV, NEB, TEV) of John 2:15 make clear the meaning of the Greek text: 'So he made a whip out of cords, and drove all from the temple area, both sheep and cattle; he scattered the coins of the money changers and overturned their tables. To those who sold doves he said ...' (NIV). For exegetical comment, see John Ferguson, *The Politics of Love* (James Clarke, 1973), 28-30.
12. Donald B. Kraybill, *The Upside-Down Kingdom* (Herald Press, 1978); Jim Wallis, *The Call to Conversion* (Lion Publishing, 1982), ch. 1.
13. For a discussion of Jesus' attitude to the power-holders of his day, see Richard J. Cassidy, *Jesus, Politics and Society* (Orbis Books, 1978).
14. Ronald J. Sider, *Christ and Violence* (Lion Publishing, 1980), 46-48.
15. Hendrikus Berkhof, *Christ and the Powers* (Herald Press, 1962), 31; Dale Aukerman, *Darkening Valley: A Biblical Perspective on Nuclear War* (Seabury Press, 1981), 78-79.
16. Ralph P. Martin, *Reconciliation: A Study of Paul's Theology* (Marshall Morgan & Scott, 1981), ch. 9; John H. Yoder, *The Politics of Jesus* (Eerdmans, 1972), 222-224.
17. John H. Yoder, *The Christian Witness to the State* (Faith and Life, 1964), 72.
18. A. Ruth Fry, *Victories without Violence* (Dennis Dobson, 1957); Elizabeth H. Bauman, *Coals of Fire* (Herald Press, 1954); Cornelia Lehn, *Peace Be with You* (Faith and Life Press, 1980); Philip Hallie, *Lest Innocent Blood Be Shed* (Michael Joseph, 1979).
19. Yoder, *Christian Witness*, 71-73.
20. 'A Blast from the Bishops', *Time*, 8 November 1982, 20.

Common Affirmations and Actions

Nuclear weapons have for the first time in history, brought adherents of the two historic Christian approaches to warfare into a single movement. In the face of the nuclear arms race, pacifists and Just War theorists are no long combating each other. We have discovered that our approaches are two ways of coming to the same conclusion; and we are thinking and working together.

We have been discovering that we have much in common. Both pacifists and Just War theorists regard the nuclear arms policies of our own government, and of other governments, as immoral. Both of us recognise that nuclear weapons are not producing security; they are rather producing fear, and thus heightened insecurity. Both of us are awed by the immensity of the evil that we are called to struggle against; and yet, despite principalities and powers, industrial infrastructure and military hardware, 'common sense' and government policy, both of us cherish the remarkable belief that God works through his children to effect his will in history – even against impossible odds.

At root, both of us – Just War adherents and pacifists alike – are driven by the deep conviction that NUCLEAR WEAPONS ARE WRONG. Our ethical positions both establish boundaries, and we will not concede that any cause is so vital or essential that we will cross these boundaries. Pacifist Christians will not kill; Just War Christians will not tolerate the killing of millions of innocent people. Even if a totalitarian, atheist enemy threatens us with immoral weaponry, we will not violate our convictions by responding in kind. Victory over our enemies is morally meaningless if, in the process of winning, we become indistinguishable from them. So Just War and pacifist Christians are, in increasing numbers, joining together to work and pray against nuclear weaponry.

But our shared ground is not simply a negative

one. Pacifist Christians and adherents of the Just War agree as well in many positive affirmations.

1. *We must repent. All* of us, whether pacifists or adherents of the Just War, are complicit in the nuclear build-up that threatens the mass irradiation of creatures and creation. Pacifist Christians have been guilty of irresponsible withdrawal from the real world; we have often been more concerned to avoid doing evil than actually, at the price of peril and ambiguity, doing good. All too often we have washed our hands of political witness; and we have seldom experimented with alternatives to violence or with concrete expressions of enemy-loving and peacemaking. Accustomed to saying a quiet 'no' and to being overlooked, we have allowed ourselves to be shunted aside as irrelevant. The powers of the world have ignored us in a way that they never ignored Jesus.

Just War Christians have been equally unfaithful to the best insights of their tradition. Instead of holding up an explicit standard by which believers could measure the policies of their governments, they have unabashedly lapsed into using the 'just war' as a slogan. *Our country always fights just wars; our means are invariably just and necessary.* (Our Christian enemies, viewing the same wars from their perspective, have generally viewed their causes and means as equally just. The most recent example of this is the Argentinians of 1982). As technology has enabled warfare to become increasingly destructive and indiscriminate, Just War adherents have seldom expressed their disapproval. Accustomed to being good citizens, Christians in the Just War tradition have been unaccustomed to saying 'no'. Instead of withdrawing like many pacifists into purist irrelevance, Just War Christians have been 'relevant' at the price of saying nothing of substance.

If God's people are to play a creative role in this late hour of history, we – of both traditions –

must turn around. We must let God heal our fears and change our minds. We must open ourselves to his gifts of faith and courage which will enable us, by challenging the accepted assumptions and military postures of our country, to say 'no'. And yet, since we ourselves are complicit in the world's nuclear predicament, we must speak humbly with those who disagree with us.

2. *We must ask questions of accepted wisdom.* Since the bombing of Hiroshima at the end of World War II, most Christians have repressed thought about nuclear weapons. Between 1965 and 1980 there was not one debate in Parliament about British nuclear policy. Most Christian groups were equally willing to suspend reflection. As our political and military leaders lulled us with comfortable words, we have accepted these without question and gone about more urgent tasks.

This easy acceptance must stop. As Just War adherents and pacifists repent, one aspect of our repentance must be the recovery of our critical faculties, which we will apply in light of Scripture to the formative slogans of our time. 'Peace through Strength' (US Air Force motto). But does the threat (and the fear) of mass destruction produce anything that the Bible means by peace? Is not Biblical *shalom* present only when there is justice, right relationships, and the absence of fear?[1] 'Deterrence has worked and will continue to work'. Admittedly there has not yet been a nuclear war in Europe. But has the absence of nuclear war really been the result of clever human contrivance (deterrence theory)? Has it rather been a gift of grace (think of all the nuclear wars by accident that we have almost had!)? Has it been a gift of time, during which the Divine 'Restrainer' (2 Thess. 2:6-7) has held back the massed forces of destruction until we come to our senses? Has he been giving us the opportunity to confess our arrogant assumptions that we can be lords of history, and to alter our policies of threat and obliteration? How much more time will he give us if we do not turn around?

As our minds begin to change and we begin to break free of the stranglehold of old slogans, we must not relax our mental vigilance. For every movement, including the Peace Movement, has its glib slogans. We must especially query any statements which will promise that, through nuclear armament or nuclear disarmament, our nation will have peace and security. In the nuclear age all policies are risky. Indeed, we Christians should have a special sensor for detecting false promises. We must be rightfully suspicious of anybody who advocates a policy which rules out suffering.

3. *Nuclear-armed nationalism is idolatrous.* Pacifists and adherents of the Just War can agree in pointing out that the nation-state would appear to be the highest good (whether consciously or unconsciously) of those who justify the possession and use of nuclear weapons. It is not the people of the nation whom they value; after a nuclear war there would be no more than 5 to 20 million Britons left.[2] Nor is it the survival of the nation in any recognisable form; in a matter of hours nuclear war would snuff out the nation's culture and democratic institutions. It rather seems to be the idea of the nation-state. In order to vindicate national independence and honour, we will do *anything,* including unleashing the powers of the cosmos upon our adversaries, in the full expectation that, as they do the same to us, only a fraction of our people will survive. We will, in short, commit a mass sacrifice. Even the vocabulary of nuclear warfare evokes worship: in the 'holocaust' (whole burnt offering) there will be millions of 'victims' (animals offered in sacrifice to a deity). The boundlessness of this sacrifice of life indicates the extent to which the nation-state, as an absolutised collectivity, has become an *idol.*[3]

Surely our fellow-believers, in their secret selves, do not believe that any human institution or cause is so sacrosanct that we will make *any* sacrifice for it. Jesus warned his disciples that they could not serve both God and earthly sources of security (Matt. 6:24). Nor can we. In what or whom do we trust: the self-absolutising idol, or the Lord, who is 'our strength and shield' (Ps. 115:9)?

4. *We must resist the dehumanisation of the enemy.* War is a product of stereotyping. It is almost inevitable when we view any group of people not as human beings but as an undifferentiated mass, hostile and threatening, who are different from ourselves. Killing a person with a name and family is difficult. So we develop faceless, collective nick-names for our enemies (Japs, Jerries, Krauts, Commies, Gooks, Argies).[4] Our media repeatedly remind us how different they are from us. And, ignoring the evils in ourselves and our allies, we fancy ourselves to be God's

agents and the enemy to be 'Antichrist'. The result is genocidal atrocities. As one Jewish scholar wrote, reflecting the agony of his own people's experience, 'Dehumanisation is an early warning of holocaust'.[5]

Christian pacifists and Just War thinkers should be alarmed that precisely this pre-holocaust dehumanising, on the part of both the West and the Russians, is now taking place. Our politicians and media feed us with facts and interpretations which reinforce our fears, and which justify growing arms expenditures and an ever more deep-seated suspicion. From their politicians and media the Russians receive a mirror-image impression of the capitalist West. We do not need to be unrealistic about the Soviet Union's military capabilities or oppressive society to recognise that *something must change* – in ourselves as well as in our enemies – if we are to avoid a holocaust in which we and they give ultimate expression to the fear and hatred that are within us.

As Christians, who have a special calling in situations of tension to 'love our enemies', we are uniquely equipped to be instruments of change. Loving our Russian enemies can take many forms, of which I suggest only three. First, we can remind ourselves of our oneness with millions of Russian people in the Body of Christ; 20 per cent of the Soviet citizens are active church members, almost twice as high as in the UK.[6] Second, we can love our Russian enemies by learning to know them personally. We can correspond with Russian believers who are eager to learn English; or we can visit them in person. In times of international tension we can use our freedom to travel to meet face-to-face the brothers and sisters, as well as the non-Christian Russians, whom our nation is dehumanising and threatening to incinerate with nuclear warheads. Tour parties of faithful Christians can go to Russia as well as to Israel! Third, we can love our Russian enemies by attempting to understand the way they think. We could, for example, develop the mental discipline of listening to the news from their perspective, of thinking how the most recent Western military innovation might affect them instead of thinking only how their weapons might affect us. These attempts to love our Russian enemies might not make much difference. But who knows? History, after all, is in God's hands, and he *commands* us to love our enemies!

5. *We have a prophetic mission.* In the nuclear age some Just War adherents and pacifists, like the ancient prophets, will be anointed for a specific task – conveying God's message to our time. There are two aspects of this prophetic ministry. One is to discern the consequences of the choices that people are making, and to state them with clarity and passion. To Hosea (10:13-14) it was clear that it was 'because you have trusted in your chariots and the multitude of your warriors [that] the tumult of war shall arise among your people, and all your fortresses shall be destroyed'. Similarly Jesus, in the agonising awareness that his Jewish contemporaries had rejected 'the way that leads to peace', warned them of the destruction which would result from their choice of military resistance to the Romans: 'A time will come upon you, when your enemies will set up siege-works against you; they will encircle you and hem you in at every point; they will bring you to the ground, you and your children within your walls, and not leave you one stone standing on another' (Luke 19:41-44 NEB). Jesus said this while he was looking down upon the 'city of peace' (Jerusalem), weeping. This is the attitude which the authentic prophets of today have as well. The prophets to ignore are those who are not compassionate.

The second aspect of the prophetic ministry is to call people to conversion – to change their hearts and minds and lives. How little faith most of us have in God's capacity to change people! The prophet Jonah, certain that the city of Nineveh was beyond repentance, fled in the opposite direction rather than confront it with a message of judgement and hope. And when the city, in response to his warning of impending catastrophe, actually repented, he was furious. Many of us would do well to meditate on Jonah's faithlessness and fury – and also on the Lord's passionate desire for his creatures to turn from the way that leads to destruction: 'And should I not pity Nineveh, that great city, in which there are more than a hundred and twenty thousand persons who do not know their right hand from their left, and also much cattle?' (Jonah 4:11).

6. *Many of us will have to make some difficult decisions.* Adherents of the Just War and pacifists are convinced that nuclear weapons are not only immoral; they are likely to be the instruments of humanity's ultimate mortal sin. Once we allow this realisation to begin to sink in,

'If all this capacity for destruction is spread around the world in the hands of all kinds of different characters – dictators, reactionaries, revolutionaries, madmen – then sooner or later, and certainly I think by the end of this century, either by error or insanity, the great crime will be committed.'

Harold Macmillan

things can never be quite the same for us again. Those of us whose churches have been concerned solely about individual sin will have to decide whether to urge pastors and fellow believers to preach and encourage discussion on this social sin. Those of us who have only expressed ourselves politically by voting in general elections will have to decide whether to be active between elections by writing to our Member of Parliament about nuclear weapons or by becoming active in a peace organisation. Those of us who have been campaigning on the life issue of abortion must decide whether our logic does not compel us to campaign on the life issue of the nuclear killing of millions of foetuses inside their mothers. For some of us, these decisions will disturb our routines, distract us from our spare-time activities, and bring us into association with new sorts of people.

For others of us, whose workaday lives are intertwined with the manufacture or handling of nuclear weapons, the decisions could have serious professional and economic consequences. Civil engineers may decide that they cannot in conscience work on nuclear-related contracts. Researchers in military-related industries may find that they can no longer morally justify their investigations. Soldiers may discover that, as nuclear weapons spread throughout the forces, they can no longer in conscience serve in ways that they had done. As a result of their Christian moral convictions, many believers in this country and abroad have left their security behind them, resigned their jobs and entered the wilderness in search of alternative employment.

What is the use of dramatic gestures such as these? Will not the nuclear-arms systems carry on without us? And why ask our families to suffer for the sake of our apparently futile expressions of moral scrupulousness? Realistically we must concede that the systems probably will continue undisturbed; and our economic suffering may well be real. However, our primary concern is not so much to be effective as to be obedient. We are concerned not with our enemy's immorality but our own. Even if our actions seem to bear no visible results we cannot choose to act otherwise. But who knows? It is *certain* that the systems will continue undisturbed if we continue to give them our support. But if we do what our consciences tell us is right and withdraw our support, changes could conceivably begin to take place.

Throughout the Bible God effects changes in ways that humans cannot anticipate. It was a lunatic gesture for Abraham to leave civilised life in Chaldea for a nomadic trek in the wilderness. But Abraham in faith believed in the God who had called him and followed his lead in obedience. The result was a mighty people and the blessing of the whole human race. Because of his faithfulness Abraham became our father; and we become his children if we do what he did (John 8:39). Modern-day successors of Abraham can – if they leave their equivalents of Chaldea – be tools of change. In their wanderings in the wilderness they will discover in the Lord, and in their families of faith, real sources of sustenance. They can also persevere in the knowledge that historically no breakthrough for any major cause has taken place without suffering. Perhaps this is a moment in history when God is calling many of us, for the sake of peace, to leave self-interest behind and to commit acts of Christian heroism!

7. *There are alternatives to the UK's nuclear policy.* Adherents of the Just War and pacifists may not know what these alternatives are. But we affirm that the Lord never places his children in a situation in which their only course of action is one of monumental immorality. The response to immorality is repentance; and repentance means not only feeling sorry for sinfulness but turning from sin to something else. For those who have sensed God's call to live without nuclear weaponry the search for that alternative is a central concern.

The search for alternatives is never easy. Customary orthodoxies are powerful. They are buttressed by tradition, respectability, and massive public funding. On the other hand, those who are working for change are fringe characters, maligned in respectable circles, abysmally funded, and engaged in an uphill struggle. Yet the work of these alternative thinkers is not only precarious; it is also of vital importance, and it must be supported by the finances and prayers of believers. Indeed, it is in alternative thinking and research that Christians will find the most appropriate avenues for involvement in society. There are several possible alternatives to the nuclear arsenal which we looked at in Part I, Study Session 5. As we search for alternatives we must also work for a shift in UK nuclear weapons policy. This could begin with some unilateral gesture, such as deferring or scrapping plans for the deployment of Trident or Cruise missiles. But in view of the dictates of Christian morality, it must go farther than that – to the rejection by the UK of all nuclear weapons, and the withdrawal of British bases to American nuclear forces. The strategic implications of these actions are complex, and cannot be discussed here. But it is worth noting that by ceasing to be a nuclear power Britain would not be espousing an unusual defence posture; it would simply be adopting a non-nuclear stance similar to that of the vast majority of the world's countries.

8. *We must face up to the possible consequences of our position.* Critics of Christian advocates of nuclear disarmament accuse us of being unrealistic. Power, they point out, is 'the major factor in international diplomacy', and nuclear weapons are our era's most formidable engines of power. When there is an imbalance of power, or a power vacuum, hostile forces will use the situation for their own advantage. 'The preservation of peace and the acceptance of limitations on nations are most likely to be achieved by the maintenance of a balance of power'.[7] Or to put it negatively, war and the extension of oppression are the probable results of a disturbance of the balance of power. If a nuclear country such as Britain abandoned its bomb, the global balance would be dangerously altered. The 'peace movement', by ignoring these realities of power, is simply being irresponsible. If we have a nuclear war, or the expansion of Soviet domination, it will have a lot to answer for.

This realist argument is a serious position, which nuclear disarmers of Just War and pacifist persuasions must take seriously. Yet it seems, even in its own terms of power and realism, to be an incomplete argument. It ignores at least four realities. First, the realist argument ignores that even if Britain renounced its nuclear weapons, it would by no means be militarily powerless. It would still possess a vast array of 'conventional' weapons with which to defend its shores and project its power throughout the world. Second, the realist argument further ignores the fact that Britain, although a major 'conventional' military power, is only a minor nuclear power. Britain's 192 strategic nuclear warheads are potent; but they seem paltry compared to the United States' 9000 warheads or the Soviet Union's 7000. If Britain unilaterally gave up her nuclear capability, it would make very little difference to the

balance of power which would continue to exist between the nuclear super-powers. Third, the realist argument ignores the possibility that a minor power such as Britain that relinquished its nuclear weapons would thereby gain another kind of power. It would gain a leverage in international diplomacy that would enable it, at this critical moment in history in which more and more nations are being tempted to acquire their own nuclear weapons, to introduce something new into a situation that is fast becoming unmanageable. By contrast, Britain's stubborn retention of its status as a second-rank nuclear power locks it into a position of powerless uncreativity.

Finally, the realist argument ignores the fact that since Hiroshima our weapons are no longer instruments of human strength; they have now come to be expressions of our ultimate helplessness. Behind the 'balance of power' in the nuclear age is thus the fear of annihilation; and this fear is immobilising. The Christian realists themselves do not know what to do. They can, of course, pour cold water on new ideas. But, imprisoned by their presuppositions about power, they cannot see any way forward other than the conventional military orthodoxy – which each year is adding thousands of new nuclear weapons to the 50,000 which already exist. Genuine realism tells us that this cannot go on forever, and that as a human family we are running out of time. Someone, in realism, must hazard something new before the bombs fall.

Unilateral nuclear disarmament by Britain would be an attempt, in an increasingly dangerous world, to begin something new. The advantages of this policy cannot be argued here;[8] but its risks must be mentioned. Even if Britain were to discard its nuclear weapons and adopt a neutral stance, there would nevertheless be a risk of nuclear attack in time of war. It would probably be less likely than at present that the attack would be all-out; but it is not impossible to conceive of one power or another destroying a few British airports to prevent its opponents from ever using them. Furthermore, in a world in which other countries would have nuclear weapons, there would continue to be the possibility of nuclear blackmail, whether by the Soviet Union or by some lesser nuclear power of the future. The threat of a Russian invasion would probably not be the greatest of Britain's worries. The offensive

capability of the Warsaw Pact has generally been exaggerated; and, according to a recent leading article in the *Times*, 'the endemic Polish crisis has decisively altered the European balance of power in the West's favour'.[9] But it is theoretically conceivable that at some point in the future the Soviet Union might attain the necessary combination of dominance over her Eastern European allies and superiority over NATO military forces necessary to over-run Western Europe and to threaten Britain. Whether the risk of nuclear obliteration would be less for the U.K. if it adopted a policy of unilateral nuclear disarmament is a matter of judgement – I believe that it would be somewhat less. But no nuclear disarmer can promise the United Kingdom a future without risk, danger and suffering.

Ultimately, however, adherents of the Just

War and pacifists are not swayed by arguments about power and risk. They advocate nuclear disarmament for Britain not because of what our enemies might do to us but because of what we might do to them. It is our own immorality that scandalises us, not our enemy's. We cannot contemplate coming before Christ in judgement with the blood of millions of innocent Russians – Christians and non-Christians alike – on our hands. Even in the unlikely event that the choice would be an extreme one – between doing something morally outrageous and losing one's national independence – we would do the latter. John Stott put it like this:

'If the issue was either using a nuclear weapon or allowing invasion, yes, I believe it would be right to permit invasion. I don't like the phrase 'better red than dead'; I would say 'better to be slaves under an alien regime than to defend our freedom immorally'. We know that freedom is possible under an alien regime: Roman occupation of Palestine may not have been as bad as Gulag in Russia, but it was pretty brutal, and yet Jesus himself was the free man.'[11]

9. *Our most important activity is prayer.* These are difficult times, and many of us – perhaps especially those of us involved in the peace movement – are conscious of our impotence. The technological, political and military forces heading for nuclear conflagration appear to be both monumental and unstoppable. In our experience the biblical teaching on 'principalities and powers' – in which malevolent spiritual forces work through earthly structures and movements – begins to take on a very concrete meaning. As the peace movement gains in political influence, we may well discover that Western democracies retain their tolerance only as long as their fundamental assumptions are not challenged. We are likely to suffer, and to lose heart.

These are times for all of us – whether adherents of the Just War or pacifists – to 'stand fast', to 'keep alert', and to 'pray at all times in the Spirit' (Eph. 6:14,18). Let us therefore make prayer our priority. Let us pray for ourselves. In our work for peace we are certain to experience intense and frequent conflict. If we reflect about this in prayer, we will discover the truth of Thomas Merton's comment that 'the root of war is fear', not only in the functionaries in Whitehall or the Kremlin, but in our own hearts.[10] Let us therefore pray that God may heal the hatred and fear in each one of us, giving us his love which casts out fear and enabling us to be faithful stewards of the time and vision which he has given us.

Let us pray for our churches, that they may be communities of peace, demonstrating to the world that Jesus is alive now, reconciling the irreconcilable and making them brothers and sisters in his family. Let us pray for our rulers, our persecutors, and our enemies. Despite the biblical injuctions to pray for these (1 Tim. 2:2; Matt. 5:44; Luke 6:28), most of us are inexperienced at this; we are far more accustomed to complain, criticise and dehumanise. In the nuclear age an incredible weight rests on the shoulders of world leaders; and their judgements are as affected by depression and dyspepsia as any of the rest of us!

Above all, let us pray the prayer which Jesus taught us: 'Thy Kingdom come!' Let us pray this not with our lips but with the whole orientation of our lives. His kingdom is here and is coming. Nothing can frustrate it. Let us live now in the 'justice, peace and joy in the Holy Spirit' (Rom. 14:17) which one day will be totally victorious.

Questions for Study and Discussion

Common Affirmations and Actions

1. Summarise the common affirmations and actions on which pacifists and Just War adherents can unite.
2. 'Is not Biblical *shalom* present only when there is justice, right relationships and the absence of fear?' Discuss the implications of this concept of peace. (You may wish to consult other sources on the Biblical concept of *shalom.*)
3. To what extent do you think the nation-state has become an idol? Would you consider it possible if the state required obedience contrary to the scriptures, that you would refuse to obey?
4. What ways does Kreider suggest to love our Russian enemies? What are your responses to these suggestions? Could you as individuals or as a group take steps in this direction?

Notes: Common Affirmations and Actions

1. Walter Brueggeman, *Living Toward a Vision: Biblical Reflections on Shalom* (United Church Press, 1976); Colin Brown, ed., *The New International Dictionary of New Testament Theology* (Paternoster Press, 1976), II, 776-783.
2. Peter Goodwin, *Nuclear War: The Facts on our Survival* (Acts and Grant, 1981), 114. Cf. Owen Greene, et. al., *London After the Bomb: What a Nuclear Attack Really Means* (Oxford University Press, 1982), 36 ff.
3. Aukerman, *Darkening Valley*, ch. 9.
4. Jesse Glenn Gray, *Warriors: Reflections on Men in Battle* (Harcourt Brace, 1959), 132-133.
5. Rabbi Marc H. Tanenbaum, in preparatory documents for International Conference on the Holocaust and Genocide, Tel Aviv, 20-24 June 1982.
6. Walter Sawatsky, *Soviet Evangelicals Since World War II* (Herald Press, 1981), 14; Nationwide Initiative in Evangelism, *Prospects for the Eighties: from a Census of the Churches in 1979* (The Bible Society, 1980), 15.
7. Graham Leonard, Bishop of London, 'The Morality of Nuclear Deterrence', lecture at St. Lawrence Jewry, London, 3 November 1982, reported in *Times,* 4 November 1982, 5.
8. Robert Neild, *How To Make Up Your Mind About the Bomb* (André Deutsch, 1981), ch. 9-10.
9. 'How the Centre Can Hold', *Times,* 4 November 1982, 15.
10. Thomas Merton, *New Seeds of Contemplation* (New Directions, 1961), ch. 16 (esp. p. 122); Kenneth Leech, *True Prayer: An Introduction to Christian Spirituality* (Sheldon Press, 1980), ch. 3.
11. John Stott in *Third Way*, February 1982, 12.

PART III

Paths to Peacemaking

Introduction to Part Three

There is a danger in exposing oneself to a volume of information on these issues – the danger of being inundated with a mass of information to the point that paralysis sets in. The issues seem to be overwhelming, the information so vast and technical, the arguments so elusive, that one's own sense of powerlessness and insignificance is intensified. Therefore, in this part we focus on ways to mobilise our concern and respond in faith to these difficult issues.

The articles were selected to give a broad spectrum of possibilities for response. They include avenues for reflection and prayer – understanding one's own capacity for violence, living a 'disarmed' life – as well as avenues for action – personal, local, national and international. They also focus on the central place of worship in the struggle, which ultimately is 'not against flesh and blood, but against the principalities, against the powers, against the world rulers of this present darkness ...' (Eph. 6:12). The final section includes a poem and prayers written for a Hiroshima Day (Feast of the Transfiguration) service. We are developing other resources – poetry, prayers, drama – on these themes. We would recommend a collection of worship materials, *My People I Am Your Security,* available from Sojourners, PO Box 29272, Washington DC 20017, USA.

We would encourage the importance of small steps, taken faithfully. Even if you cannot devote a lot of time and energy to peacemaking, you can make a significant contribution.

Consider the following beginning steps:

- Join a peace organisation. There are a wide variety of peace groups working in different areas, with different priorities. We found it to be beyond the scope of this guide to describe the various groups. We would encourage you to find out about the organisations in your area. The addresses of some of the major ones are listed at the end of this section.

- Keep the importance of peacemaking before your congregation. Plan several services around themes of peace, biblical attitudes towards enemies, dealing with fear, etc. Join with other churches in your area in a joint service for Hiroshima Day or Remembrance Sunday.

- Stock your church bookstall with books on peace themes. If your church doesn't have a bookstall, perhaps you could start one.

- Become better informed on the factors which contribute to war and peace, on government policy, on Christian teaching on war. The bibliography at the end of the section is a starting point for topics discussed in this study guide.

- Set aside one time in the week to pray together as a family or with a group of friends for peace in the world. This is a good way to make children aware of peacemaking. Pray for any situations of conflict with which you are concerned – personal, local, and national as well as global.

- Join with people around the world in praying for peace. At midday many people are offering the 'Prayer for Peace' (printed below) for one minute. This means there is a continuous vigil of prayer around the world.

Prayer for Peace

Lead me from death to life, from falsehood to truth.
Lead me from despair to hope, from fear to trust.
Lead me from hate to love, from war to peace.
Let peace fill our heart, our world, our universe.

Personal Pilgrimage

A pilgrimage towards seeing peacemaking as an integral part of renewal, by Peter Price

'News on film is only news for one day. Next day it is history.' So read an advertising slogan. The impact of one day's film has had a significant influence on the history of my life. Two news films, presented on different days, but in the same period of the late sixties, stand out clearly in my mind. One was of a little Vietnamese girl, screaming in pain, her clothes burning, running from the village which had just been subjected to a napalm attack. The other, a picture of a burnt-out street of houses in Belfast. These two pictures remain clear 'stills' in my mind; they caused me to ask the question which van Gogh asked when he was ministering to the degraded miners of Borinage – 'O God, what has happened to man?'[1] For me, these pictures marked the unconscious beginning of a pilgrimage, a conversion to seeing peacemaking as an integral part of Christian penitence and renewal.

A few days after the burning of the street in Belfast I was in a part of that city with a Christian minister, amid the tiny back-to-back houses that formed his parish. We found ourselves knocking on the doors of boarded-up buildings; houses condemned by the housing authorities. Inside were refugees, families whose homes on the near-by mixed Catholic and Protestant housing estates had been burned down. We talked to them, shared their ordeal as they described how armed men had forced them to leave, and how their neighbours had cried as they stood by, helplessly watching the burnings. At that moment there was no bitterness towards those who had been their neighbours; there was confusion, regret, anger, and a feeling of powerlessness and futility towards the perpetrators of violence. For me, at that moment, the men of violence were there to be angry with, and to hate. My 'closed-system' thinking told me that sin had led them into hatred and violence. It closed the book. It was simple; they were sinners. I did not have to think about the sense of injustice, the overwhelming frustration of powerlessness; the pain of unemployment, of inadequate housing, the sense of being manipulated, all contributing to the meaninglessness that caused the sin, expressed through violence, to emerge.

'Britain's Vietnam'

Someone once referred to Northern Ireland as 'Britain's Vietnam'. I have never been to Vietnam, but I have been many times to Northern Ireland since 1968. I have seen destruction of community; the desolation of cities, the polarisation of ordinary men and women like you and me into armed camps, potentially capable of destroying one another. Children who have never known anything but 'the troubles'; children just as bitterly destroyed in their spirit as the Vietnamese girl in her painful misery. Children condemned to exist in a perpetual atmosphere of suspicion, destroying like cancer the very fabric and structure of God-given life.

Slowly I began to realise that what lay at the heart of a localised conflict such as Vietnam or Northern Ireland lies at the heart of all potential international and national conflicts. Man, in his suspicion, fear and anger, moves swiftly into hatred, constructing barricades beginning with wood and stone and escalating inexorably to Polaris and Cruise missiles. For a long time I ascribed such feelings, when encountered, to 'others'. I could not acknowledge within myself that the suspicion, fear and anger I experienced towards others, often fellow Christians, were, in essence, the very reactions and emotions given vent to on a community, national and international scale.

In the aftermath of a particularly painful time of conflict and anger within my own relationships with others, with whom I shared ministry, a time in which it was more important to 'be right' than to love, I found myself devastated by some words of Thomas Merton's in his *Seeds of Contemplation*. He was writing about pride, spiritual pride, the danger of becoming isolated in self-satisfaction, of thinking of oneself as a 'prophet of God' or a man with a mission to reform the world. The words that spoke to me were these: 'I must look for my identity, somehow, not only in God but in other men. I will never be able to find myself if I isolate myself from the rest of mankind as if I were a different kind of being.'[2] In my pilgrimage towards seeing peacemaking as an integral part of renewal, these words were crucial. They led me into recognising the full force of some other words from Thomas Merton:

'*So instead of loving what you think is peace, love other men and love God above all. And instead of hating the people you think are warmakers, hate the appetites and the disorder in your own soul, which are the causes of war. If you love peace, then hate injustice, hate tyranny, hate greed — but hate these things* in yourself, *not in another.*'[3]

Identification

For me there are still enormous difficulties to be resolved, forgiveness to be given and received. However, what for me began as an external issue, has now become both internal and external, an identification. For me, spiritual renewal has brought about a heightened awareness of my identity with the self-centred, self-destructive, God-hating humanity which Christ came to confront with love and power. I recognise a continuing need to know the reality of a love-centered, life-saving, humanity-loving God in a deeply personal way. My whole life must be one of repentance, the whole character of my life a conversion experience, turned around and transformed. My Christian hope is that as a consequence of such a transformation, I will have the capacity to enjoy changed relationships with the rest of humanity. I am called to 'love my enemies'. 'Love one another as I have loved you.' This means loving as he loved, forgiving as he forgave, imparting peace as he imparted peace. In order to maintain the reality of that relationship and lifestyle I am encouraged to experience renewal with an ongoing 'encounter of the Third Kind', in the Holy Spirit, an encounter that makes my life a continued renewal, in love, forgiveness, concern for

friends and enemies, and above all God's will. The ultimate Christian hope is resurrection. The daily Christian experience is that of dying. To follow Jesus still means taking up the cross 'day by day'.

Political implications

Insight often comes when it is least expected. I was staying for a few days with the Community of Celebration at Cumbrae. During my time there I picked up a copy of *Sojourners,* the magazine of a community in Washington committed to a biblical perspective on the political events of our time and on the role of the church in the world. I found articles asking questions in respect of nuclear weapons – 'Can the use of these weapons be reconciled with the gospel?' 'Can their existence be reconciled with the command "Love your enemies?"' Slowly, I began to realise that the arguments that I had relied upon for my security and non-involvement were not Christian at all. I had believed the moral lie 'if we are attacked we should retaliate'. I had seen its practical futility in the streets of Belfast in a localised conflict. I had failed to grasp the horrendous implications of the nuclear weaponry that could now destroy in one war several major cities at a time. My theology of conversion and renewal had stopped short of where I stood in relation to such issues. I believed opinions on such matters to be private and personal. The title 'Prince of Peace', given to Jesus, was highly personalised, with vague stirrings of some eschatological consummation, but irrelevant to the present. The question now being pressed upon my conscience was – is there any way in which I as a Christian can accept this situation?

In one of his last speeches, Earl Mountbatten said ... 'In the event of a nuclear war there will be no chances, there will be no survivors – all will be obliterated.'[4] Einstein wrote, 'When we released the energy from the atom, everything changed except our way of thinking. Because of that we drift towards unparalleled disaster.' The compilers of the Vatican II report said 'the dangers of world destruction through nuclear weapons compels us to undertake an evaluation of war with an entirely new attitude ...' Billy Graham, whose 'change of heart' with respect to the nuclear arms issue was prompted by his visit to Auschwitz, said, 'Is a nuclear holocaust inevitable if the arms race is not stopped? Frankly, the

answer is almost certainly yes … I think many Christians are only just beginning to see that the nuclear arms race is an entirely new factor in human history, and that we cannot be complacent about it, or treat it as just another minor issue. We need to educate the Christian community about the moral and ethical issues that are involved.'[5]

For me, the beginning of an answer to these questions was summed up in these words from 'A Call to Faithfulness'[6], a statement of concern issued by Christians of many denominations in the United States: 'The Church's preaching of the gospel in our day must make it clear that a turn to Christ will lead us from the acceptance of nuclear weapons, so that converts become known as peacemakers. The Church's public witness must be marked by costly action, following the leadership of one who was willing to bear the burden of peacemaking in a hostile world. Nurtured by Christ's love, his Church must "bear all things, believe all things, endure all things".'

For me, part of that call to faithfulness is a recall to the realisation that God's command to man to 'fill the earth and subdue it' is a call to stewardship and not exploitation. Such stewardship brings with it a responsibility, not only for the environment, but for humanity, whether believing or unbelieving, enemy or friend. Translating the nuclear menace into our own experience can be dangerously over-simplified, but an attempt must be made.

Practical implications

Britain's nuclear strike forces are based in the shadow of Lincoln Cathedral, and in the Holy Loch. Submarine rockets and bombers that have the capacity to wipe out over thirty major cities in one strike, are kept on stand-by. In practical terms, this would mean that within the target areas in the Soviet Union, some twenty million people would be killed in a single strike. Soviet retaliation would produce devastation of cities here, too, Glasgow and Lincoln among them. The fine edifice of Lincoln Cathedral, bearing witness to 'Christ the Prince of Peace' would be a nuclear dust bowl. Can we imagine for a moment what it would be like in that moment when all the enemies of the world had destroyed one another, not to mention their neighbours? Christ would stand at that point of history and say, 'Did you have a part in helping to destroy all my children?' Per-

haps the excuses would come 'Well, what could we have done? Everything was so complex. We were helpless, we trusted those in authority. I suppose we helped pay for the weapons, but surely, you said ... "give to Caesar the things that are Caesar's ..."'

And Jesus might answer, 'Verily I say unto you, anything you did unto the least of my brethren, you did it unto me.'

All pilgrimages have stopping-off places; mine, so far, has brought me to a realisation that at the heart of all human conflict is fear, suspicion, anger, leading to hatred and destruction. The same forces that exist in systems and ideologies, exist in me. For me, the way back is through penitence and renewal; for the church as a whole it is through this process, too. Repentance leads inexorably to responsibility and action, not from a point of judgement, but of shared guilt and failure to recognise Jesus as he is, the Lamb who was slain beginning his reign. For me, the pilgrimage continues in response to my heart's desire, 'Your kingdom come on earth ...'

Notes: Personal Pilgrimage
1. *van Gogh* (Thames and Hudson, 1958).
2. Thomas Merton, *Seeds of Contemplation* (Anthony Clarke Books, Wheathampstead, 1972), 40.
3. Ibid., 94.
4. *A speech by Earl Mountbatten of Burma on 11th May, 1979,* published by World Disarmament Movement in association with United Nations Association.
5. *Sojourners,* August 1979.
6. Sojourners Nuclear Pack, *A Call to Faithfulness.*

Rev. Peter Price is Vicar of St. Mary Magdalene, Addiscombe, Croydon, Surrey. He was formerly a chaplain at Scargill House.

Batiks by the Scottish artist Morag MacDougall, inspired by an eye-witness account of the hours immediately after the dropping of the A-bomb on Nagasaki. He particulary remembered seeing a woman in a running position one leg lifted from the ground but completely dead, charred and burnt like a macabre statue. 'That image fixed itself on my mind and adding a child into the woman's arms, came to represent the dreadful sufferings that war brings to the innocent victims of war. The patterns in the background, which are traditional Japanese ones, taken from Japanese prints are used to represent the woman's life and environment being thrown into confusion by the A-bomb.'

The Churches for Peace

Anglican:
We condemn the subjection, intimidation and manipulation of people by use of violence and the threat of violence and call Christian people everywhere ... to take with the utmost seriousness the questions which the teaching of Jesus places against violence in human relationships and the use of armed force by those who follow him, and the example of redemptive love which the Cross holds before all people. (Lambeth Conference, 1978)

Baptist:
We affirm that we stand for peace and reconciliation among all nations, and we call on all governments of the world to stop production of, and trading in the weapons of war, conventional and nuclear. (Baptist World Alliance, 1978, endorsed by Baptist Union Assembly, London, 1979)

Methodist:
We affirm our judgement that the development and use of all nuclear weapons is abhorrent to the Christian conscience and therefore call on her Majesty's Government to phase out the British dependence on all forms of nuclear deterrence. (British Methodist Conference, 1978)

Quaker:
The existence of the international arms trade horrifies us, and we reiterate our belief that it is morally wrong ... We ask for further efforts by Friends to reach beyond the armaments industry to the roots of conflict, committing themselves resolutely and with patience to the search for non-violent solutions. Our hearts go out to all those working for peace in Ireland. (Yearly Meeting Epistle, 1977)

Roman Catholic:
The most faithful disciples of Christ have been builders of peace, to the point of forgiving their enemies, sometimes even to the point of giving their lives for them. Their example marks the path for a new humanity no longer content with provisional compromises but instead achieving the deepest sort of brotherhood. (Pope John Paul II, 1979)

United Reformed Church:
The Assembly urges H.M. Government ... to press for reductions in stock-piles of nuclear and conventional weapons; to investigate the possibilities of redirecting some of our own arms expenditure into areas of social need at home and into world development abroad; to set up research projects into the use of unarmed units in civil conflicts and in certain other confrontations where at present armed units are used in default of any alternative being available. (General Assembly, 1979)

Leaflet issued by the Fellowship of Reconciliation

'I Was Told It Was Necessary'

An interview with a military chaplain who served the Hiroshima and Nagasaki bomb squadrons.

In August, 1945, Fr. George Zabelka, a Catholic chaplain with the U.S. Army air force, was stationed on Tinian Island in the South Pacific. He served as priest and pastor for the airmen who dropped the atomic bombs on Hiroshima and Nagasaki.

He was discharged in 1946. During the next 20 years he gradually began to realize that what he had done and believed during the war was wrong, and that the only way he could be a Christian was to be a pacifist. He was deeply influenced in this process by the civil rights movement and the works of Martin Luther King, Jr. and Mahatma Gandhi.

In 1972 he met Charles C. McCarthy, a theologian, lawyer, and father of 10. McCarthy, who founded the Center for the Study of Nonviolence at the University of Notre Dame, was leading a workshop on nonviolence at Zabelka's church. The two men fell into the first of several conversations about the issues raised by the workshop. Some time later, Zabelka reached the conclusion that the use of violence under any circumstances was incompatible with his understanding of the gospel of Christ.

Now retired, Fr. Zabelka gives workshops on nonviolence and assists in diocesan work in Lansing, Michigan. The following is a recent interview with Zabelka, conducted by McCarthy.

The Editors
Sojourners Magazine

Charles McCarthy: Father Zabelka, what is your relationship to the atomic bombing of Hiroshima and Nagasaki in August, 1945?

Fr. Zabelka: During the summer of 1945, July, August, and September, I was assigned as Catholic chaplain to the 509th Composite Group on Tinian Island. The 509th was the atomic bomb group.

McCarthy: What were your duties in relationship to these men?

Zabelka: The usual. I said mass on Sunday and during the week. Heard confessions. Talked with the boys, etc. Nothing significantly different from what any other chaplain did during the war.

McCarthy: Did you know that the 509th was preparing to drop an atomic bomb?

Zabelka: No. We knew that they were preparing to drop a bomb substantially different from and more powerful than even the "blockbusters" used over Europe, but we never called it an atomic bomb and never really knew what it was before August 6, 1945. Before that time we just referred to it as the "gimmick" bomb.

McCarthy: So since you did not know that an atomic bomb was going to be dropped you had no reason to counsel the men in private or preach in public about the morality of such a bombing?

Zabelka: Well, that is true enough; I never did speak against it, nor could I have spoken against it since I, like practically everyone else on Tinian, was ignorant of what was being prepared. And I guess I will go to my God with that as my defense. But on Judgment Day I think I am going to need to seek more mercy than justice in this matter.

McCarthy: Why? God certainly could not have expected you to act on ideas that had never entered your mind.

Zabelka: As a Catholic priest my task was to keep my people, wherever they were, close to the mind and heart of Christ. As a military chaplain I was to try to see that the boys conducted themselves according to the teachings of the Catholic Church and Christ on war. When I look back I am not sure I did either of these things very well.

McCarthy: Why do you think that?

Zabelka: What I do not mean to say is that I feel myself to have been remiss in any duties that were expected of me as a chaplain. I saw that the mass and the sacraments were available as best I could. I even went out and earned paratroop wings in order to do my job better. Nor did I fail to teach and preach what the Church expected me to teach and preach – and I don't mean by this that I just talked to the boys about their sexual lives. I and most chaplains were quite clear and outspoken on such matters as not killing and torturing prisoners. But there were other areas where things were not said quite so clearly.

McCarthy: For example?

Zabelka: The destruction of civilians in war was always forbidden by the Church, and if a soldier came to me and asked if he could put a bullet through a child's head, I would have told him absolutely not. That would be mortally sinful. But in 1945 Tinian Island was the largest airfield in the world. Three planes a minute could take off from it around the clock. Many of these planes went to Japan with the express purpose of killing not one child or one civilian but of slaughtering hundreds and thousands and tens of thousands of children and civilians – and I said nothing.

McCarthy: Why not? You certainly knew civilians were being destroyed by the thousands in these raids, didn't you?

Zabelka: Oh, indeed I did know, and I knew with a clarity that few others could have had.

McCarthy: What do you mean?

Zabelka: As a chaplain I often had to enter the world of the boys who were losing their minds because of something they did in war. I remember one young man who was engaged in the bombings of the cities of Japan. He was in the hospital on Tinian Island on the verge of a complete mental collapse.

He told me that he had been on a low-level bombing mission, flying right down one of the main streets of the city, when straight ahead of him appeared a little boy, in the middle of the street, looking up at the plane in childlike wonder. The man knew that in a few seconds this child would be burned to death by napalm which had already been released.

Yes, I knew civilians were being destroyed and knew it perhaps in a way others didn't. Yet I never preached a single sermon against killing civilians to the men who were doing it.

McCarthy: Again, why not?

Zabelka: Because I was "brainwashed"! It never entered my mind to publicly protest the consequences of these massive air raids. I was told it was necessary; told openly by the military and told implicitly by my Church's leadership. To the best of my knowledge no American cardinals or bishops were opposing these mass air raids. Silence in such matters, especially by a public body like the American bishops, is a stamp of approval.

The whole structure of the secular, religious, and military society told me clearly that it was all right to "let the Japs have it." God was on the side of my country. The Japanese were the enemy, and I was absolutely certain of my country's and Church's teaching about enemies; no erudite theological text was necessary to tell

Father George Zabelka in 1945

me. The day-in-day-out operation of the state and the Church between 1940 and 1945 spoke more clearly about Christian attitudes toward enemies and war than St. Augustine or St. Thomas Aquinas ever could.

I was certain that this mass destruction was right, certain to the point that the question of its morality never seriously entered my mind. I was "brainwashed" not by force or torture but by my Church's silence and whole-hearted cooperation in thousands of little ways with the country's war machine. Why, after I finished chaplaincy school at Harvard I had my military chalice officially blessed by the then Bishop Cushing of Boston. How much more clearly could the message be given? Indeed, I was "brainwashed"!

McCarthy: So you feel that because you did not protest the morality of the bombing of other cities with their civilian populations, that somehow you are morally responsible for the dropping of the atomic bomb?

Zabelka: The facts are that seventy-five thousand people were burned to death in one evening of fire bombing over Tokyo. Hundreds of thousands were destroyed in Dresden, Hamburg, and Coventry by aerial bombing. The fact that forty-five thousand human beings were killed by one bomb over Nagasaki was new only to the extent that it was one bomb that did it.

To fail to speak to the utter moral corruption of the mass destruction of civilians was to fail as a Christian and a priest as I see it. Hiroshima and Nagasaki happened in and to a world and a Christian Church that had asked for it – that had prepared the moral consciousness of humanity to do and to justify the unthinkable. I am sure there are church documents around some place bemoaning civilian deaths in modern war, and I am sure those in power in the church will drag them out to show that it was giving moral leadership during World War II to its membership.

Well, I was there, and I'll tell you that the operational moral atmosphere in the church in relation to mass bombing of enemy civilians was totally indifferent, silent, and corrupt at best – at worst it was religiously supportive of these activities by blessing those who did them.

I say all this not to pass judgment on others, for I do not know their souls then or now. I say all this as one who was part of the so-called Christian leadership of the time. So you see, that is why I am not going to the day of judgment look-

ing for justice in this matter. Mercy is my salvation.

McCarthy: You said the atomic bombing of Nagasaki happened to a church that "had asked for it." What do you mean by that?

Zabelka: For the first three centuries, the three centuries closest to Christ, the Church was a pacifist church. With Constantine the Church accepted the pagan Roman ethic of a just war and slowly began to involve its membership in mass slaughter, first for the state and later for the faith.

Catholics, Orthodox, and Protestants, whatever other differences they may have had on theological esoterica, all agreed that Jesus' clear and unambiguous teaching on the rejection of violence and on love of enemies was not to be taken seriously. And so each of the major branches of Christianity by different theological methods modified our Lord's teaching in these matters until all three were able to do what Jesus rejected, that is, take an eye for an eye, slaughter, maim, torture.

It seems a "sign" to me that seventeen hundred years of Christian terror and slaughter should arrive at August 9, 1945, when Catholics dropped the A-bomb on top of the largest and first Catholic city in Japan. One would have thought that I, as a Catholic priest, would have spoken out against the atomic bombing of nuns. (Three orders of Catholic sisters were destroyed in Nagasaki that day.) One would have thought that I would have suggested that as a minimal standard of Catholic morality, Catholics shouldn't bomb Catholic children. I didn't.

I, like the Catholic pilot of the Nagasaki plane, "The Great Artiste," was heir to a Christianity that had for seventeen hundred years engaged in revenge, murder, torture, the pursuit of power, and prerogative violence, all in the name of our Lord.

I walked through the ruins of Nagasaki right after the war and visited the place where once stood the Urakami Cathedral. I picked up a piece of a censer from the rubble. When I look at it today I pray God forgives us for how we have distorted Christ's teaching and destroyed his world by the distortion of that teaching. I was the Catholic chaplain who was there when this grotesque process that began with Constantine reached its lowest point – so far.

McCarthy: What do you mean by "so far"?

Zabelka: Briefly, what I mean is that I do not see that the moral climate in relation to war inside or outside the church has dramatically changed much since 1945. The mainline Christian churches still teach something that Christ never taught or even hinted at, namely the just war theory, a theory that to me has been completely discredited theologically, historically, and psychologically.

So as I see it, until the various churches within Christianity repent and begin to proclaim by word and deed what Jesus proclaimed in relation to violence and enemies, there is no hope for anything other than ever-escalating violence and destruction.

Until membership in the Church means that a Christian chooses not to engage in violence for any reason and instead chooses to love, pray for, help, and forgive all enemies; until membership in the Church means that Christians may not be members of any military – American, Polish, Russian, English, Irish, et al.; until membership in the Church means that the Christian cannot pay taxes for others to kill others; and until the Church says these things in a fashion which the simplest soul could understand – until that time humanity can only look forward to more dark nights of slaughter on a scale unknown in history. Unless the Church unswervingly and unambiguously teaches what Jesus teaches on this matter it will not be the divine leaven in the human dough that it was meant to be.

"The choice is between nonviolence or nonexistence," as Martin Luther King, Jr. said, and he was not, and I am not, speaking figuratively. It is about time for the church and its leadership in all denominations to get down on its knees and repent of this misrepresentation of Christ's words.

Communion with Christ cannot be established on disobedience to his clearest teachings. Jesus authorized none of his followers to substitute violence for love; not me, not you, not Jimmy Carter, not the pope, not a Vatican council, nor even an ecumenical council.

McCarthy: Father Zabelka, what kinds of immediate steps do you think the church should take in order to become the "divine leaven in the human dough"?

Zabelka: Step one should be that Christians the world over should be taught that Christ's teaching to love their enemies is not optional. I've been in many parishes in my life, and I have found none where the congregation explicitly is called upon regularly to pray for its enemies. I think this is essential.

I offer you step two at the risk of being considered hopelessly out of touch with reality. I would like to suggest that there is an immediate need to call an ecumenical council for the specific purpose of clearly declaring that war is totally incompatible with Jesus' teaching and that Christians cannot and will not engage in or pay for it from this point in history on. This would have the effect of putting all nations on this planet on notice that from now on they are going to have to conduct their mutual slaughter without Christian support – physical, financial, or spiritual.

I am sure there are other issues which Catholics or Orthodox or Protestants would like to confront in an ecumenical council instead of the facing up to the hard teachings of Christ in relationship to violence and enemies. But it seems to me that issues like the meaning of the primacy of Peter are nowhere near as pressing or as destructive of Church credibility and God's world as is the problem of continued Christian participation in and justification of violence and slaughter. I think the church's continued failure to speak clearly Jesus' teachings is daily undermining its credibility and authority in all other areas.

McCarthy: Do you think there is the slightest chance that the various branches of Christianity would come together in an ecumenical council for the purpose of declaring war and violence totally unacceptable activities for Christians under all circumstances?

Zabelka: Remember, I prefaced my suggestion of an ecumenical council by saying that I risked being considered hopelessly out of touch with reality. On the other hand, what is impossible for men and women is quite possible for God if people will only use their freedom to cooperate a little.

Who knows what could happen if the pope, the patriarch of Constantinople, and the president of the World Council of Churches called with one voice for such a council? One thing I am sure of is that our Lord would be very happy if his Church were again unequivocally teaching what he unequivocally taught on the subject of violence.

Reprinted with permission from Sojourners *Magazine, August 1980*

My People, I Am Your Security

A Nuclear Prophecy

In the summer of 1978, David H. Janzen, a member of the New Creation Fellowship in Newton, Kansas, fasted and prayed about a Christian witness against the arms race. He was given what he felt to be a prophecy from the Lord, and shared it with his fellowship, who confirmed it. It was then shared with a group meeting at the Mennonite World Conference held in Wichita, Kansas, in July of that year; that group felt led to share it with the whole general assembly. Following is the prophecy.

My people, proclaim to your governments and your neighbors that you do not need armaments for your security.
I am your security. I will give the peacemakers glory as I defended and glorified my own defenseless son, Jesus.
My kingdom is international.
I am pleased that my children gather all around the globe to give allegiance to one kingdom. My kingdom is coming in power.
No powers, not even the powers of nuclear warfare can destroy my kingdom.
My kingdom is from beyond this earth.
The world thought it had killed Jesus, Jesus through whom I have overcome the world. Therefore, be not afraid.
You are a gathering of my kingdom;
My kingdom will last forever.
Taste the first fruits now;
Embrace the international fellowship in Christ and praise me together.
Do not fear the nuclear holocaust.
Do not panic or take unloving short cuts to fight the armaments monster.
I go before you to do battle.
This is a spiritual battle, the battle to destroy war.

Do not attempt to fight this battle on your own.
Fear, guilt, and anger will make you spiritual prisoners of the enemy if you fight on your own authority.
Learn to hear my voice. Learn to be at unity with those who love me.
I will lead and protect my army.
I will coordinate the battle in many nations.
I want to show you where the idols of this age are hidden.
Learn where are the missile silos, the bomb factories, the centers of military command, the prisons for dissenters.
Understand that those who bow down to fear, trust in these idols for salvation.
Stand beside their idols and proclaim my liberating kingdom. Invite them to share your life in me. Perfect love must be your weapon, for perfect love casts out fear.
If you obey my call, you will be persecuted, misunderstood, powerless.
You will share in my suffering for the world, but I will never abandon you. You belong to my international, eternal kingdom.
Do not say time is running out. Do not threaten or despair.
I am the Lord of time. There is no time to seek the world's approval, but there is time to do what I will lay before you.
By my mercy I have extended time.
I extended time for a perverse human race when I called Noah.
I lengthened the time of repentance by sending my prophets.
I have averted nuclear disaster many times for you.
Jesus offers you all time, time to repent and come to me.
Obey my call and there will be time to do what I am laying before you.

Now is the time.
I want you to learn who around the world has
refused to bow down to the god of fear or
worship weapons of terror.
Hold hands around the world with my
soldiers, my prisoners.
Pray for each other and share my strength
with them.
I love those who put their trust in me and
will put joy in their hearts.
There is time to build my kingdom.
There is time to protest armaments and to
build a spiritual community for those who
turn from the idols of fear.
Call them to join you in the security that
flows from Father, Son, and Spirit, my
community, given for you.
My seed is planted in every one of my children;
It is waiting to break the husks of fear that it
may grow toward my son's light.
I did not plant my Spirit in Russians or
Americans, Arabs or Israelis, capitalists
or communists that they might destroy
each other, but that they might recognize
my image in each other and come together
in praise of their Creator's name.
My beloved children,
Share the burden of my heart, know my love
so that you may learn to die for one
another.
There is time to do this.
Trust me and I will sustain you within my
kingdom forever.

Questions for Study and Discussion

Pilgrimage in Peacemaking

'Personal Pilgrimage'

1. Peter Price speaks of his pilgrimage as a 'conversion to seeing peacemaking as an integral part of Christian penitence and renewal'. Do you share his conviction about the central place of peacemaking for a Christian?
2. How do you respond to Merton's statement, 'Instead of loving what you think is peace, love other men and love God above all. And instead of hating the people you think are warmakers, hate the appetites and the disorder in your own soul, which are the causes of war. If you love peace, then hate injustice, hate tyranny, hate greed – but hate these things *in yourself,* not in another'? Do you agree that peacemaking must be an inward pilgrimage as well as an outward, active one? If so, how do you begin such a pilgrimage? Are you aware of your own capacity for violence? If so, how does this affect your attitude towards those you consider to be 'warmakers'? How does it affect your action for peace?
3. Reflect on your position with respect to your pilgrimage in peacekeeping. Members of the group may wish to share some of the experiences, thinking, and reading that have brought them to their present position.

'I Was Told It Was Necessary'

4. According to Fr. Zabelka how had the church prepared the moral consciousness of humanity for the use of nuclear weapons? What is your response to his experience? In the light of his experience, do you feel the church has a responsibility to oppose the present nuclear arms race?
5. What are the hallmarks of church membership that Fr. Zabelka sees as necessary if the church is to take a significant stand against escalating violence and destruction? Where do you think *your* church is in relation to these hallmarks?
6. What is your response to Zabelka's idea of an ecumenical council for the purpose of declaring 'that war is totally incompatible with Jesus' teaching and that Christians cannot and will not engage in or pay for it from this point in history on'. What do you think would be the effect of such a council, if it were to happen?

'My People, I Am Your Security'

7. The prophecy focuses on the importance of recognising the powerful spiritual forces underlying the arms race, and in trusting in God's love and power to overcome them. How does this perspective influence your response to the present world situation?
8. The prophecy also emphasises that Christ's kingdom is international, and encourages us to deepen our solidarity with people in all nations who worship the God of peace and reject the god of fear. How could this solidarity be deepened? What could your church or group do to facilitate the recognition of God's image in people of other nationalities, political persuasions, religious beliefs?

Responses of Faith

The Peace Tax Campaign

The Peace Tax Campaign addresses the dilemma of 'praying for peace while paying for war'. Initiated in 1977 by Stanley Keeble, it has received widespread support from the Society of Friends (the Quakers), from a number of prominent people, including peers, bishops and MPs, as well as from a large popular following. The aims of the Campaign are stated as follows: 'In simple terms the Campaign aims to persuade the government to introduce legislation to enable individuals to be exempt from paying for military expenditure. Here it must be made clear that there is no suggestion of opting out of paying taxes, or of seeking personal financial gain. The intention is that a special Peace Fund should be established, into which tax payers who wish will be able to pay the proportion of their taxes which would otherwise have gone towards military expediture.' In more formal terms, the aim of the Campaign is as follows: 'To establish the statutory right whereby all who object to paying for war or military preparations on the grounds of conscience or profound conviction shall have that part of their tax payments, which is equivalent to their compulsory contribution to military expenditure, paid into a Peace Fund and used exclusively for non-military peace-making purposes.'

The Campaign is built on the realisation that modern warfare is conducted not primarily with large numbers of conscripts, but with technologically advanced weapons which are at present being amassed and are financed by taxes collected by the Inland Revenue from the adult population. Though the right to conscientious objection to compulsory military conscription has been legally recognised in Britain since 1916, there is no exemption from paying for war. Thus, those who conscientiously oppose war, and refuse to participate in the military, are put in the compromising position of paying others to do what they themselves cannot do in good conscience.

The Campaign's pamphlet expresses this ethical dilemma succinctly: 'In law it is recognised that to hire a killer is to be guilty of murder as to carry out the killing personally. By extension, to provide a small military elite with the means to fight a modern technological war is to share an equal responsibility for the ensuing slaughter.' Thus, the purpose of the Campaign is 'not necessarily to seek from all people their personal rejection of arms, welcome though that would be, but to gain support for a new freedom of conscience, so that those who believe war to be wrong shall no longer be forced to pay for the preparation of this evil'.

Their proposal, subject to further consideration, is that the Peace Fund be established by Act of Parliament and that this Act would provide for the appointment of a governing body of trustees to administer it in accordance with that constitution.' Some of the proposed uses of the Fund are the building of trust and understanding between individuals and nations through a variety of means: 'the fostering of travel exchanges; the exchange of news and personnel responsible for cultural programmes; the establishment and maintenance of Peace Research Departments; the funding of local and national peace workers; the development of peace education courses at primary, junior, secondary and university levels; the establishment of internationally staffed monitoring agencies; practical assistance in suitable peace promotion or tension reduction projects; assistance in funding conversion projects from the manufacture of armaments to alternative production; and the establishment of volunteer units ready to work anywhere in the world where emergency needs calling for non-military peaceful action might arise.'

In their clear and concise pamphlet the Peace

Tax Campaign sets out several options for determining the proportion of tax that is used for military purposes, and suggests possible courses of action for those who wish to support the campaign. For this information write to: Margaret and Stanley Moore, The Secretaries, Peace Tax Campaign, 26 Thurlow Road, Leicester, LE2 1YE.

(Quoted excerpts from Peace Tax Campaign pamphlet, available from the above address.)

Peace Camps

The Women's Peace Camp at Greenham Common and the People's Peace Camp, Molesworth are witnesses for peace at the bases which are proposed sites for American Cruise Missiles. Members of the Molesworth Peace Camp describe their objectives in their pamphlet:

'We are here as non-violent witnesses for peace. We do not believe that peace can be achieved by preparing for war, but rather by working for trust and understanding instead of fear. The camp is a focal point in the struggle to make sure that cruise missiles do not come to Britain. Fear feeds the Arms Race (the bombs produced daily have the destructive power of a million tons of TNT). The money that is spent on the Arms Race could be used to clear the world's slums, to end hunger, to prevent avoidable disease and to teach every child to read and write. Just two weeks of military spending every year would provide the money needed. We are not against the American people, but against the US Government's siting of their missiles on our land; this puts us at a terrible risk. Yet Britain has no control over the launching of these missiles. To threaten to use weapons against children, women, men and animals of any country is immoral. The weapons that might come to Molesworth could kill 60 million people. We reject the threat to carry out mass murder in our names.'

'Already more than half of the British people do not want American bases here. We do not intend to allow more of them on our land. Many top military experts, including the late Lord Louis Mountbatten, think that nuclear weapons have no military purpose. Already nine out of ten Britons believe that they may well die in a nuclear war, but many of them think that we are too weak to stop our government from playing leapfrog with death. However, we believe that to stop cruise missiles from coming is an achievable aim. When plans for cruise missiles are cancelled people will gain new confidence – the game can be stopped – our rulers can be persuaded to do as people wish. The peace camp provides one of the means to achieve this.'

'We are with people everywhere – in America, Japan and all parts of Europe who are resisting oppression and nuclear violence ... The Peace Camp will encourage basic crafts and creative arts. We wish to see the land of the base once more growing crops and flowers. We meet regularly for prayer and also seek to join in prayer locally. We will hold non-violent Direct Action workshops and special action days. We will reach out to the community and talk, write and act to spread our convictions.'

A resident of the camp writes: 'We receive many visitors here – including Christian groups and individuals who see us as a focal point for work to bring the arms race to a halt. We would like our message to reach the ears of many more Christians – especially to see articles from and about us in the churches' press. We believe that Christ's message clearly condemned the use of violence to meet violence and that He made it clear that to threaten wrong to others is the same morally as to do that wrong. We ourselves pledge non-violence as our lifestyle and the need to live more simply that others may simply live. We remember the warnings of Jeremiah that God's people should trust in Him, not in our own force and violence against oppression.'

The Peace Camp is sponsored by the Fellowship of Reconciliation, Green CND, Quaker Peace and Service, Greenham Common's Women's Peace Camp for Life on Earth, Christian CND, Pax Christi and many local groups and individuals. Members of the camp are available to speak at meetings and to write articles explaining their stand. For more information write to: People's Peace Camp, Old Weston Road, Brington, Huntingdon, Cambs PE17 5LP. Telephone contact Clopton 257.

NOTE: Since the original writing of this book, a peace camp has also been established at Faslane on the lower Clyde.

'As possessors of a vast nuclear arsenal we must also be aware that not only is it wrong to attack civilian populations but it is wrong to threaten them as part of a strategy of deterrence.'

U.S. Catholic Bishops

Letters to Parliament

One way of expressing your concern about Britain's current defence policy is to write to your Member of Parliament. Some useful guidelines for writing such a letter are listed below:

1. Address:

    Mr. J. Bloggs, MP (or Rt. Hon. J. Bloggs, MP) House of Commons, London SW1.

2. Be brief:

    Just long enough to put the points you want to put. Don't try to say too much – single out ideas you think most telling or topical.

3. Heading:

    It may be useful to put a heading to your letter – 'Disarmament', or whatever aspect of disarmament you wish to stress. The recipient will certainly read the heading, even if he doesn't read the whole letter – though nearly all MPs will read it right through. Any MP will take serious note, if and when, he is receiving letters on disarmament at the rate of hundreds per month.

4. Your own words:

    A short question from some famous person may be useful to make a point, but it is essential that you give your own personal convictions, expressed in your own words – preferably with some reason(s) to support

them. MPs take note of all views reasonably expressed. If you know the MP concerned is already worried about present policies then you could write to express your appreciation and support. The numbers of letters received reflect the importance of the subject in the public mind. A pro-disarmament MP must be able to stand up in the House, when the occasion arises, and say 'I have received 1000 letters demanding disarmament . . .' or whatever the numbers may be.

5. Questions:

    It may be useful for a change to ask a question especially when writing to someone with a special responsibility, such as a party leader or spokesman on defence.

6. Holidays:

    You can still write when Parliament is not in session. They get letters sent on – and may have more time to deal with them!

The Fellowship of Reconciliation has a scheme whereby volunteers are invited to write on a continuing basis to selected MPs, expressing their own views on the subject of disarmament in their own way. If you would like to join in the scheme please write for a list of names to Alan Litherland at the following address:

Alan Litherland,
37 Arlington Road,
DERBY DE3 6NZ

(Guidelines for letter-writing, courtesy of Alan Litherland, Fellowship of Reconciliation).

The Lucas Aerospace Corporate Plan

Britain is one of the world's leading arms manufacturers and traders, with customers all over the globe. Approximately 500,000 people are involved directly or indirectly in military production. Of these, around 75-80,000 work mainly on export contracts, with another 90,000 peripherally involved. Taking into account civil servants engaged on defence projects (some of whom work, not for the MoD, but for the Department of the Environment!), and including a further 400,000 plus jobs in ancillary industries, there are more than 1,000,000 people in Britain and abroad dependent on British military spending. By way of comparison, Britain has only 85,000 doctors and 600,000 teachers.[1]

'Arms production, and the jobs that it provides, is a central feature of the UK economy. Most of the high priority research and development carried out in British universities and research establishments is directed towards military objectives, a large tranche of the developments and production of the growing electronics industry has military application, and many of the tedious assembly jobs carried out in companies with names familiar in any household are for incorporation into weapons or military back-up systems.'[2]

The myth that arms expenditure is necessary to sustain employment is very widespread. The single most important argument against it has come through the alternative Corporate Plan launched by workers at Lucas Aerospace in 1976. Lucas Aerospace (LA) is a division of the large British multinational company Lucas Industries. It employs over 12,000 workers and operates over 17 different sites throughout the UK. LA produces a wide range of electrical and mechanical systems with aerospace application. About 50% of its products are in the defence sector, and 80% of its output is on contract with the Government.

Between 1970 and 1974, the company shed 5,000 jobs. The shop stewards, who had formed themselves into a Combine Committee in 1972, decided that industrial action should be combined with a political and economic response to the threatened redundancies. The result was the publication, in 1976, of the Alternative Corporate Plan of the Lucas Aerospace Combine Shop Steward's Committee. The idea was to propose alternative products that could be made using the company's existing plant and workforce, with the real possibility of employment expansion in the future and the minimum of re-training. From hundreds of ideas put forward, one hundred and fifty were proposed for further development. It had not been stressed that the ideas should be non-military, but this was the unanimous outcome, and consequently social utility was given a high profile in the final report.

The proposals contained in the plan covered six product areas:[3]

1. *Oceanics:* including a valve operating system, nodule gathering mechanisms, and marine agriculture vehicles and equipment.

2. *Telechiric machines:* unmanned cable-operated submersible vehicles for helping to exploit the energy, mineral and food resources of the sea.

3. *Transport systems:* including a prototype hybrid power-pack incorporating an internal combustion engine, generator, batteries and an electric motor. This would use much less fuel than an ordinary petrol engine, and would virtually eliminate pollution.

4. *Braking systems:* existing systems could be greatly improved by the addition of the 'electric magnetic dynamometer'.

5. *Alternative energy sources:* especially wind power and solar heating projects.

6. *Medical equipment:* from life-support systems (pacemakers, kidney machines, etc.) right down to a hob-cart for the benefit of children suffering from the crippling disease of spina-bifida.

The idea of the Lucas Plan was to achieve a balance between financial viability, social utility and job creation. The Lucas planners argued convincingly that although the plan needed Government back-up to get it off the ground, this was an infinitely better use of public money than subsidising redundancies.

The response of the Lucas management was negative. They claimed that the plan was unprofitable and unworkable, even though their own studies on some of the products had shown that they could be highly profitable. As a contrast, the response to the plan amongst economists, the press and technical experts was positive. The real worry of the management, according to the workers, was that the proposals threatened their hitherto unchallenged right to plan products.

Moreover it also challenged aspects of the division of labour, and showed that it was possible to balance social needs against profitability. The management, by contrast, were *solely* interested in profitability.

Meanwhile Government support was also limited. At the time some Labour Ministers were keen on the plan, but were unable to gain financial support in the face of IMF imposed public expenditure cuts. Elements of the Trade Union movement were also negative. They were dis-

turbed about the idea of a Shop Stewards Combine by-passing the formal planning mechanisms of Trade Union organisation. So for political reasons the plan has floundered, though few have questioned its economic or technical validity. However, positive steps have been taken. Firstly, a *Centre for Alternative Industrial and Technological Systems* (CAITS) has been set up by the Lucas shop stewards at the North East London Polytechnic. The idea has been to develop, expand and publicise the Lucas proposals; to promote the concept of socially useful production; and to encourage similar workers' plans in many other industries. The ideas for the Alternative Plan are being taken up all over the world. Workers at Vickers at Barrow-in-Furness and other arms factories have been working on other plans, and practical proposals for government mechanisms (including an arms conversion enabling bill based on model US legislation) to facilitate the concrete development of the Lucas products, are being considered within the labour movement.

Perhaps even more importantly, one of the more sensational ideas in the plan (a road-rail vehicle which could potentially revolutionise freight transport in Britain and the Third World) is being developed independently as a focus for promoting the Lucas initiative as a whole. Details are available from CAITS.

Altogether, the Lucas Aerospace Plan represents possibly the most exciting development in practical peacemaking of the last hundred years. There is plenty of scope for public involvement in debate, in funding and in publicising the proposals. Further information is available from CAITS, or from Campaign Against the Arms Trade (see p. 117 for addresses).

Questions for Study and Discussion

Responses of Faith
'The Peace Tax Campaign'
1. Do you feel that those who conscientiously oppose war should have an alternative to contributing financially to warmaking? What is your personal response to the possibility of establishing and contributing to such a Peace Fund? In the absence of such a fund, would you consider other means to avoid paying for warmaking?

'Peace Camps'
2. The presence of Peace Camps at proposed missile sites provides a visible focal point for witness against the arms race. How do you respond to that kind of action? Make a list of ways your group might make visible your feelings on this issue. Are there nuclear facilities in your area that you would like to make a stand against?

'The Lucas Aerospace Corporate Plan'
3. How do you feel about Britain's economic dependence on the manufacture and trade of arms? What steps could be taken to break this dependence, and to encourage the implementation of plans such as the Lucas proposal?

Notes: The Lucas Aerospace Corporate Plan

1. 'Choices' – a Campaign Against the Arms Trade pamphlet.
2. 'The Battle For Jobs' in *War Lords* – a Counter Information Services Report on the UK Arms Industry, 26.
3. Transport & General Workers' Union, *Military Spending, Defence and Alternative Employment*. Statement issued by the General Executive Council for the Twenty-Seventh Biennial Delegate Conference (London, TGWU, 1977), 4-6.

Rooted in Worship

Rooted in Worship by Val Nobbs

Jesus said, 'Blessed are the peacemakers, for they shall be called sons of God.'[1] To make peace involves a great cost, it may mean the sacrifice of all that is most dear to us. Daniel Berrigan, in his book *No Bars to Manhood* writes:

'There is no peace because there are no peacemakers. There are no makers of peace because the making of peace is at least as costly as the making of war – at least as liable to bring disgrace and death in its wake.'[2]

We are caught between our desire for peace and our desires and plans for a normal, happy life. We want to finish our education, to have a happy home and family, to succeed in our career, to do the best for our children. And the years go by, and the nuclear arsenals grow and, for all our hopes, peace does not come. The disruption to our well-ordered, normal lives is too great, the price is too high, we dare not risk everything we have worked and hoped for. In short, we are afraid. So where do we find the strength and courage to make peace, to step outside the bounds of what is normal, to dare to follow Christ into the heart of the conflict?

To be true peacemakers, our lives must be rooted in prayer and worship. To live non-violently takes tremendous courage and a strength that we alone can never possess: not to hurt back when we are hurt, not to lash out in anger when we feel betrayed, not to rise up in indignation and defend ourselves when we have been misunderstood. If we would make peace, we must let God disarm us. We must journey inwards and face the fears and conflicts within ourselves. In solitude we can let God strip away our defences until we are left standing before him in vulnerability.

'We should let ourselves be brought naked and defenceless into the centre of that dread where we stand alone before God in our nothingness, without explanation, without theories, completely dependent upon his providential care, in dire need of the gift of his grace, his mercy and the light of faith.'[3]

We are full of fears that keep us suspicious and isolated, unable to reach out and touch each other. Behind all these fears lies our fear of death. In solitude we can let God free us from the crippling effects of these fears. Solitude is a kind of death, a letting go of all things. It is the place we can let God disengage us from the cares and preoccupations of day to day living that seem so important. We can draw apart enough to see life with a clearer vision. The temptation is to go mad with those we are trying to save. If we draw apart for a while we can let God shape us from within; we can find a meaning for our lives that is a response to God's call to our freedom. We need no longer be moulded and shaped by the forces of this present world.

'What am I? I am myself a word spoken by God. Can God speak a word that does not have any meaning?

Yet am I sure that the meaning of my life is the meaning God intends for it? Does God impose a meaning on my life from the outside, through event, custom, routine, law, system, impact with others in society? Or am I called to create from within, with him, with his grace, a meaning which reflects his truth and makes me his "word" spoken freely in my personal situation? My true identity lies hidden in God's call to my freedom and my response to him. This means I must use my freedom in order to love, with full responsibility and authenticity, not merely receiving a form imposed on me by external forces, or forming my own life according to an approved social pattern, but directing my love to the personal reality

109

of my brother, and embracing God's will in its naked, often unpenetrable mystery.'4

This is vitally important. If we are to take on the powers of this world and do battle with them, we must be free of them in our own lives. We cannot owe any allegiance to them but must be wholly dependent upon God. Then, whatever happens to us, wherever our path leads us, we will have nothing to lose, nothing to fear.

In solitude we see that the forces that lead to war lie within us, the seeds of all hatred and violence can be found in our own hearts. We are inextricably bound up in the sin of the world, we share the common guilt for the injustice and oppression. We must acknowledge our corporate sin, our sharing in the guilt of humanity, and repent. We are a part of the human drama, we cannot divorce ourselves from it and would not want to. In solitude we continually confess our part in the injustice and are continually forgiven and made new.

Our search for peace does not end in solitude. We cannot stay alone. Our search for peace brings us together, in worship of him who is our peace. As God disarms us we learn to be open and non-defensive with each other. As we find God at our centre we can create the space to invite others in to us, no longer as threats to be kept at arms length but as precious gifts to be loved and cherished.

God is calling many of us, his people, to live close enough together that our differences affect each other. We are becoming involved in one another's lives. As this happens we become increasingly aware of the discord and selfishness within ourselves. We have set our hearts towards living non-violently, in the midst of our differences and disagreements; giving ourselves to the creative resolution of conflicts. We are seeking a love that is greater than our differences, a commitment not to give up the struggle to keep loving each other when we are tempted to despair. As we come together in worship we draw near to the source of our hope, we proclaim whom we trust and wherein lies our security. Over against the idolatry of the Bomb we reaffirm our trust in the Prince of Peace.

To make peace is to engage in a spiritual battle, to take up arms against the hosts of wickedness in high places.

'For we are not contending against flesh and blood, but against the principalities, against the powers, against the world rulers of this present darkness, against the spiritual hosts of wickedness in the heavenly places.'5

St. John, in his first Epistle, tells us that the whole world is in the power of the evil one. It is easy to lose sight of this when we come to worship, to act as if our worship happens in a vacuum and is divorced from life. It is important for us to regain a sense of what we are *not* worshipping, as well as coming to reaffirm our trust in a loving God. For the first century Christians, worship was a political act. When they came together in worship of Christ they were deliberately choosing to refuse to worship the emperor – it was often a matter of life or death. We too must be aware of the choice we are making, we must proclaim Jesus as Lord over against the Bomb.

Historian, Arnold Toynbee has said, 'Nationalism is the religion of 90% of the people'.6

As we come together in worship we denounce the lie, and expose it as we acknowledge our oneness as children of the same heavenly Father. He has broken down all barriers. In Christ, there is neither Russian nor American, Communist nor Capitalist, East nor West, 'Free World' nor Iron Curtain, rich nor poor, but all are one. If we would truly follow the Prince of Peace it is no good condemning the armed forces or the submarine commanders; it is not enough to talk of peace with Russia but to hate those in our own country who do not share our views. Love is our meaning. Christ has called us out of our divisions and hostilities to be reconciled to one another in him.

'To reconcile man with man and not with God is to reconcile no one at all.'

We are not interested in creating further divisions, in building empires or founding ideologies, nor in 'enlightening' others to our point of view or winning people over to our side. Our first allegiance is to Christ and his Kingdom; we have been called to love and serve God and our brothers and sisters.

As we come together as God's children, the Body of Christ here on earth, we are reminded that the image of God dwells in all people and that:

'all the nuclear weapons delivery systems of the world, point towards a target that comprehends

'It is no use to have the greatest and best army in the world if the people are dying from hunger.'
José Napoleón Duarte,
President of El Salvador,
1981

the least of all who are his. The slain Brother would be there with every brother and sister, with every terrified child as the slower ghastliness of radiation sickness spreads across the continents.'[9]

In worship, we reaffirm our obedience to Christ and proclaim our hope in a God who raises the dead. We cannot be just another voice clamouring for survival. Julian of Norwich once said of Christ, 'He said not, "Thou shalt not be tempested", but "Thou shalt not be overcome".' To follow Christ is not the guarantee of a divine insurance policy against nuclear holocaust. Our hope goes beyond survival. Where three of God's people in ancient Babylon refused to bow down and worship a golden image of the king, Nebuchadnezzar was understandably furious. He threatened them with death.

'If you do not worship the image you shall immediately be cast into a burning fiery furnace; and who is the god that will deliver you out of my hands?'[10]

The king was given the following answer:

'If it be so, our God whom we serve is able to deliver us from the burning fiery furnace. But if not, be it known to you, O king, that we will not serve your gods or worship the golden image which you have set up.'[11]

Our God is able to deliver us from a nuclear holocaust; but even if he does not we will not bow down and worship the Bomb. If we are to involve ourselves deeply in the peace movement, we need to find this hope within ourselves.

'When protest simply becomes an act of desperation, it loses its power to communicate anything to anyone who does not share the same feelings of despair.'[12]

In worship, our faith is strengthened in the loving purposes of a God in whose hands the greatest evil is turned to good. At the heart of the suffering of Auschwitz, Hiroshima, and the Cross we find Jesus, the Central Victim – God present with us in the midst of our darkness, bringing hope out of despair and resurrection out of death. May we know this hope to which God has called us – a God who has:

'raised Christ from the dead and made him sit at his right hand in the heavenly places, far above

all human targets: Jesus. The cold warriors of West and East, with no eyes to glimpse the "enemy multitudes", see the One least of all. But Christians must understand that no nuclear weapon is aimed without pointing toward him. "As you did it to one of the least of these my brethren you did it to me."'[8]

To plan to kill our brother is to plan to crucify Christ. He would be the central victim in the midst of the annihilation.

'Each victim he would know; each passion, each death he would feel. He in whom God has drawn near would be there in a thousand infernos with *all rule and authority and power and dominion, and above every name that is named, not only in this age but also in that which is to come; and he has put all things under his feet and has made him the head over all things for the church, which is his body, the fulness of him who fills all in all.'13*

Worship Materials

**Prayers/Meditations for use on August 6th:
Feast of Transfiguration/
Feast of Disfiguration**

(These are intercessory prayers, written for use in a liturgical form of worship, but may be adapted for use in other services).

Lord, we ask you to have mercy on us as we seek to follow you. We ask forgiveness for the times when, as a church we have condoned bloodshed and fighting. We ask you to forgive us today for the times we stand as silent onlookers while our nation prepares for war. We pray, in your mercy, you would give us grace to follow you, to put our trust in you, not in weapons of war and our military might, that you would teach us to love our enemies. Work in us a willingness to be broken and vulnerable, to walk your way of suffering love.

Lord, we pray for your church ... (Spontaneous prayers may be offered by numbers of the congregation.)

Lord, in your mercy, hear our prayer.

Lord, we confess to you that we are more on the side of the rich and powerful than the poor, to whom you gave the kingdom of heaven. We admit to you that by our birth we are part of the world's privileged few. We ask you to forgive us for being part of an unjust economic system that exploits the poor for our own sake. We confess to you our sale of arms to poor countries for our own economic gain. We ask you to forgive us and lead us in the ways of justice and truth. Help us to see all people, not as enemies to be feared and hated, but as brothers and sisters to be loved and cared for.

Lord, we pray for the nations of the world ...

Lord, in your mercy, hear our prayer.

Lord, we confess to you the violence and anger in our own hearts. We see that the roots of all war and discord lie within us. We confess to you the times we have failed to love our friends, our neighbours, our own relatives and family. We admit to you the broken relationships in our lives and ask for your reconciling love to work among us. We thank you that in Christ you reconciled us to yourself and gave us the ministry of reconciliation.

Lord, we pray for this (*town/city*) in which we live, our families, and friends ...

Lord, in your mercy, hear our prayer.

Lord, we confess to you our own bewilderment and lack of understanding in the face of suffering. We pray for your forgiveness for the suffering we inflict on others. We ask your mercy on those who suffer as a result of war. For those who today still suffer as a result of the bombs dropped on Nagasaki and Hiroshima. We thank you for your son, Jesus, who shared our suffering, our loneliness, our agony, our death. Thank you that by being one with us he redeemed us, by bringing God into our lives and us to God. Give us grace to live out your suffering love.

Lord, we pray for the sick and suffering ...

Lord, in your mercy, hear our prayer.

Lord, it seems that every bit of our lives is touched by a bit of death. In every satisfaction there is an awareness of its limitations, in every friendship, distance and in all forms of light, the knowledge of surrounding darkness. We thank you that this awareness of death can point us beyond this life in expectation to the day when our hearts will be filled with joy, when there will be no more death and no more pain.

Lord, we pray for the departed, especially remembering those who have died in war ...

Lord, in your mercy, hear our prayer.

Father, we offer you ourselves, our world, our families and friends. All the things that concern us. All that we bring with us to this place as we've come to worship you. We ask you to accept our prayers and strengthen us to live the life of your son, Christ our Lord. Amen.

Val Nobbs: Cumbrae 8 August 1981
© Celebration Services (International) Ltd., 1981

Transfiguration.

'Now there are only two radiations we move
*   toward:*
*   the radiation of Christ or the radiation of the*
*   atom.'*

                                    Brother Roland Walls

August 6   Feast of Transfiguration

Behold the Christ
the mountain vision
radiating the splendour of God
revealing the potential of humanity.
Behold the radiant God man:
fulfilment of Moses' law
fulfilment of Elijah's prophecy.
Behold, o man
and be struck dumb
by unspeakable glory.

On the mountain –
humanity glorified
but in the valley
humanity writhes
in the wasted shape
of the small boy
by dumb demons driven.

Transfiguration's mountain vision
is robed in human flesh
as the radiant Jesus descends
touches the twisted shape,
driving tormentors away,
restoring humanity's glory
completing transfiguration.

August 6   Feast of Disfiguration

Behold Nagasaki, Hiroshima
their mountains splendid
with atomic fire
their peoples transfigured
by atomic blast,
their survivors
writhing in the valley
begging some splendid Christ
to touch and make whole.

Behold the radiant Bomb:
defying the law
ignoring the prophets.
Behold, o man
and be struck dumb
by unspeakable terror.

Feast
of Disfiguration
borne not of the mountain's vision
but of dumb demons
refusing to see in other –
sister and brother
seeing only
enemy

building always walls
to keep the other out:
Democracy/Communism
Black/White
Male/Female
Rich/Poor
Christian/Moslem
build the walls
behind them pile defences
enough to obliterate the other
before they obliterate us,
until some jumpy finger
in a moment of dumb
panic
pushes the button
and the smoking timbers
of our civilised lives
lie charred heaps
against the fouled sky.

August 6   Feast of Transfiguration/Feast of Disfiguration

'Now there are only two ways to walk:
Toward the radiance of the transfigured Christ
or the radiance of the Bomb.'

Towards the radiance that descends
to touch, to heal, to restore
or
towards the radiance that descends
to defend, to murder, to destroy.

Towards the radiance that glorifies,
or the radiance that vaporises.

'This day I set before you life and death,
a blessing and a curse:
Choose this day
whom you will serve.'

Martha Keys Barker: 2 August 1980

© Celebration Services (International) Ltd., 1980

Questions for Study and Discussion

Rooted in Worship

1. Peacemaking involves facing our own fears and conflicts. During the time between group sessions reflect on your fears and conflicts. What fears are raised by the idea of leading a vulnerable, or a defenceless life? In what ways does the fear of death influence your life? This may be a matter for private reflection and prayer, or if desired, may be shared in the group.

2. What are some of the external forces or powers that shape our lives and 'impose a meaning on (my) life from the outside'? To what powers do we pay allegiance – nationality? Class distinctions? Economic status? Success? How do we free ourselves from the worship of these gods? To choose to worship Christ means the rejection of our allegiance to other gods.

3. In your church's worship could you increase the awareness of the forces and powers that you have chosen not to worship? What difference would this make to your worship?

4. Discuss the implications of the statement: 'But Christians must understand that no nuclear weapon is aimed without pointing toward him (Christ). "As you did it to one of the least of these my brethren you did it to me".'

5. According to the article, where is our source of hope? Discuss the importance of this hope in dealing with the issues that are raised in the study.

6. Read the poem and prayers which focus on the issues raised in the course. If you wish, write your own reflections in the form of a poem, prayers or drama.

Notes: Rooted in Worship

1. Matthew 5:9.
2. Daniel Berrigan, *No Bars to Manhood* (Bantam Books, 1970), 49.
3. Thomas Merton, *Contemplative Prayer* (Darton, Longman and Todd Ltd., 1973), 85.
4. Ibid., 84.
5. Ephesians 6:12.
   (Other references to principalities and powers can be found in Rom 8:38 f, 1 Cor 2:8, 1 Cor 15:24-26, Eph 1:20 f, Eph 2:1 f, Eph 3:10, Col 1:16, Col 2:15).
6. Bart Gavigan, *The Violent Christians (proposed series for television)*.
7. Thomas Merton, *Faith and Violence* (University of Notre Dame Press, 1968), 148.
8. Dale Aukerman, *Darkening Valley – A Biblical Perspective on Nuclear War* (Seabury, 1981), 48.
9. Ibid., 48.
10. Daniel 3:15.
11. Daniel 3:17, 18.
12. Thomas Merton, *Faith and Violence*, 147.
13. Ephesians 1:20-23.

What Happens Next?

In this last session the whole group evaluates the study and considers ways to respond to the concerns raised by it. This could contain several elements, giving the most time to considering possible courses of action. Assuming the group has two hours, the time may be allotted as follows:

A. Evaluation of the Course (15 minutes): Each person states what they found helpful, what they did not find helpful, and makes suggestions for improvement. One person writes these on a blackboard or large sheet of paper.

B. Sharing (15 minutes): Each person shares

briefly new insights they have gained, attitudes that have changed, or personal growth that has happened during the course.

C. Looking Ahead (1 hour)
1. Brainstorming: Use the blackboard or large sheet of paper to list ideas for action and response. Consider all possibilities. Don't be limited by practical considerations at this stage and don't discuss ideas. Just let them flow. Consider what peacemaking means in every arena of life: for individuals, for families, for churches, for communities, for nations.
2. Discussion: Once you've written down all your ideas, allow time for discussion. Divide your list into those that are possible at the present, and those that are long-term goals. Discuss which ones you feel are the most exciting and possible for your group. Consider which might be commitments for individuals, and which for the group.
3. Goal-Setting: Decide on at least one definite step for the group to take. Decide a strategy to begin in this direction, what steps must be taken, and assign tasks to those who are able to carry them out. If the group is to continue to meet, decide on a time for the next meeting.

D. Prayer and Worship (30 minutes): It is our hope that through these sessions members of the group have grown in their understanding of themselves, their appreciation of others in the group, and in commitment to peacemaking. Use this time to give thanks for the understandings that have emerged, to give expression to the concerns that have been raised, and to ask God's help and guidance for the future. If group members have written reflections, prayers or poems as part of the previous session, they may wish to share them here.

115

Glossary

BALLISTIC MISSILE: Any missile, which after launch, travels without power to its target.

ICBM: (Inter-continental Ballistic Missiles) are usually launched from silos buried in the ground, and have very long ranges.

KILOTON: The equivalent of 1000 tons of TNT, usually used to measure the power of a nuclear bomb.

MARV (Manoeuvrable Re-entry Vehicle) warheads: The next generation after MIRVs, these re-entry vehicles can manoeuvre to confuse defensive missiles. Re-entry vehicles are now being developed with 'Technical Guidance Systems' that allow them to home in on their targets with extremely high accuracy.

MEGATON: The equivalent of 1000 kilotons. One 3-megaton bomb, a moderate size weapon, has 230 times the power of the bomb that destroyed Hiroshima.

MIRV (Multiple Independently Targeted Re-entry Vehicle) warheads: In space the warhead splits into a number of separate 'Re-entry Vehicles' that can all travel to different targets. This allows one missile to attack more than one target and has superseded MRVs as it makes anti-missile defence even more difficult.

MRV (Multiple Re-entry Vehicle) warheads: When the missile gets into space the warhead splits into a number of separate 'Re-entry Vehicles' which may carry a nuclear explosive charge. These vehicles re-enter the atmosphere and all travel to the same target. MRVs were introduced to penetrate early anti-missile defence systems and are now considered obsolete.

RAD (Radiation Absorbed Dose): Since different particles absorb different levels of radiation, this measures the amount of radiation absorbed per rem given out. Human flesh absorbs almost exactly one rad per rem.

REM: Measure of energy content of radiation. Used to measure the amount of radiation required to cause particular biological damage. Each person receives a few tenths of a rem per year from background sources. There are a variety of opinions about how much more than this dosage is dangerous.

SILO: An underground chamber, housing a missile ready to be fired.

STRATEGIC MISSILE: A weapons system designed to attack targets in the enemy's homeland.

TACTICAL WEAPON: A weapon with low-yield explosive power, used in fighting by troops.

THEATRE WEAPON: Intermediate range weapon; (but not intermediate in yield) intended for use in particular theatre or region of war, e.g. Western Europe. (Does not include weapons pointed at the USA or the USSR.)
'Tactical', 'theatre' and 'battlefield' are terms which are often used loosely to refer to non-strategic weapons.

WARSAW PACT: Started in 1955. Includes the USSR, Bulgaria, Czechoslovakia, the German Democratic Republic, Hungary, Poland, and Rumania. (Albania was originally a member, but withdrew in 1968.)

Appendix of Peace Organisations

Anglican Pacifist Fellowship, St. Mary's Church House, Bayswater Road, Headington, Oxford OX3 9EY

American Peace Groups

    Centre for Peace & Conflict Studies, Wayne State University, Detroit, Michigan

    Project Ploughshares, Conrad Grebel College, Waterloo, Ontario NZL 3G6, Canada

    The Riverside Church, 490 Riverside Drive, New York, 10027, 212 749 7000

    Sisters of St. Joseph of Peace, 1302 18th Street N.W., Washington, DC 20036

    War Tax Alternatives, c/o 430 Montreal Street, Victoria BC V8V 127, Canada

    World Peace Tax Fund, 2111 Florida Avenue N.W., Washington, DC

Armament and Disarmament Information Unit, c/o Science Policy Research Unit, Mantell Building, University of Sussex, Falmer, Brighton BN1 9RF

British Council of Churches, 2 Eaton Gate, London SW1W 9BL, 01-730 9611

British Freeze Campaign, United Nations Association, 3 Whitehall Court, London SW1A 2EL

Campaign Against the Arms Trade, 5 Caledonian Road, London N1 9DX

Campaign for Nuclear Disarmament

    Christian CND, c/o Peace & Justice Resource & Information Centre, St. John's Church, Princes Street, Edinburgh

    Edinburgh CND, c/o Trades Council, Pacardy Place, Edinburgh

    European CND, 227 Seven Sisters Road, London N4 2D

    National CND, 11 Goodwin Street, London N4 2D

    Scottish CND, 420 Sauchiehall Street, Glasgow G2 3JD, 041-331 2878

    Youth CND, see Edinburgh CND

Centre for Alternative Industrial and Technological Systems (CAITS) NELP, Longbridge Road, Dagenham, Essex RM8 2AS

Christian Action, 15 Blackfriars Lane, London EC4

Committee on Poverty & Arms Trade, 5 Caledonian Road, London N1 9X, 01-278 1976

Council for Arms Control, 5 High Street, Windsor SL4 1LD

Council for Christian Approaches to Defence and Disarmament, 86 Leadenhall Street, London EC4A 3DH

European Peace Groups

    Eirene, International Christian Service for Peace, Engerser Str. 74b, D-5450 Neuwied, W. Germany

    International Dept. Christian Peace Conference, Prague 1, Jungmannova 9, Czechoslovakia 248866, 248536

    International Peace Council, (IKV) Netherlands, Postbus 18747, 2502 ES 's-Gravenhage, The Netherlands 070 469756

    Ploughshares Fund, Church & Peace, Ringstr. 21, 6331 Schoeffengrund, W. Germany 06445/1375 or 7496

Fellowship of Reconciliation, 9 Coombe Road, New Malden, Surrey KT3 4QA

International Institute for Strategic Studies, 23 Tavistock Street, London WC2E 7NQ

International Voluntary Service, Methodist Central Hall, Tollcross, Edinburgh 031-229 7318

Iona Community, 18 Walmer Crescent, Glasgow G51 1AT 041-427 6731

Irish Peace Groups

    Commission for Justice & Peace, 169 Booterstown Avenue, Blackrock, Co. Dublin (885021)

    Corrymeela Centre, Ballycastle, Co. Antrim

    Glencree Reconciliation Centre, Bray, Co. Wicklow (860963)

    Irish Council of Churches, 48 Elmwood Avenue, Belfast BT9 6AZ 0232 663145

London Mennonite Centre, 14 Shepherds Hill, London N6 5AQ

Medical Campaign (Edinburgh), Centre for

Human Ecology, Edinburgh.

Medical Campaign Against Nuclear Weapons, 23a Tenison Road, Cambridge CB1 2DG

National Peace Council, 29 Great James Street, London WC1N 3ES 01-242 3228

Northern Friends Peace Board, 30 Gledhow Wood Grove, Leeds LS8 1NZ

Parents for Survival
(Edinburgh) Lorna Dyer, 86 Morningside Drive, Edinburgh 031-447 8148
(Glasgow) 37 Camphill Avenue, Glasgow G42

Pax Christi, St. Francis of Assisi Centre, Pottery Lane, London W11 4NQ

Peace Advertising Campaign, P.O. Box 24, Oxford OX1 3JZ

Peace Education Network, c/o FOR, 9 Coombe Road, New Maldon, Surrey KT3 4QA

Peace Pledge Union, Dick Sheppard House, 6 Endsleigh Street, London WC1

Peace Prayer, 'The Caravan', 197 Piccadilly, London W1, 01-803 9690

Peace Tax Campaign
26 Thurlow Road, Leicester LE2 1YE
S. Keeble, Allet, Truro, Cornwall

Quaker Peace and Service, Friends House, Euston Road, London NW1 2BJ 01-387 3601

Roman Catholic Justice & Peace Commission
(National) 38/40 Eccleston Square, London SW1V 1PD 01-834 5138
(Scotland) 28 Rose Street, Glasgow G3 6RE 041-333 0238

School of Peace Studies, University of Bradford, Bradford BD7 1DP

Scottish Campaign Against Trident, see Scottish CND

Scottish Conv. Peace & Disarmament, 16 Woodlands Terrace, Glasgow G3 6DF, 041-332 4946

Shaftesbury Project Study Group on War

and Peace, c/o 8 Oxford Street, Nottingham NG1 5BH

Soviet Peace Commission, 23 Profsovwznaya Street, Moscow 117418, USSR

Stockholm International Peace Research Institute, Sveavägen 166, S-113 46 Stockholm, Sweden

United Nations Association
(Edinburgh) 44 Frederick Street, Edinburgh 2 041-248 3244
(London) 3 Whitehall Court, London SW1A 3EL

War Resisters International, 55 Dawes Street, London SE17

World Disarmament Campaign, 21 Little Russel Street, London WC1 4HF, 01-242 3486
(There are local groups for many of these organisations which can be contacted at the above addresses).

Bibliography

Aukerman, Dale. *Darkening Valley: A Biblical Perspective on Nuclear War* (Seabury, 1981).

Bainton, Roland H. *Christian Attitudes Toward War and Peace* (Abingdon, 1960).

Bishop, Peter D. *A Technique for Loving: Nonviolence as Practical Politics* (SCM Press, 1981).

Calder, Nigel. *Nuclear Nightmares: An Investigation into Possible Wars* (Penguin, 1981).

Campbell, Duncan. *Warplan UK: The Truth about Civil Defence in Britain* (Burnett Books, 1982).

Clark, Robert E. D. *Does the Bible Teach Pacifism?* Foreword by J. Stafford Wright (Marshall, Morgan and Scott, 1983).

Cox, John. *Overkill: The Story of Modern Weapons,* rev. ed. (Penguin, 1981).

Eller, Vernard. *War and Peace from Genesis to Revelation* (Herald Press, 1981).

Ellul, Jacques. *Violence* (Mowbrays, 1978).

Ferguson, John. *Disarmament: The Unanswerable Case* (Heinemann, 1982).

Ferguson, John. *The Politics of Love* (James Clarke, 1982).

Freedman, Lawrence. *Britain and Nuclear Weapons* (Macmillan, 1980).

Greet, Kenneth. *The Big Sin* (Marshall, Morgan and Scott, 1982).

Holmes, Arthur, ed. *War and Christian Ethics* (Baker Book House, 1975).

Kraybill, Donald. *Facing Nuclear War* (Herald Press, 1982).

Kreider, Alan. 'Should Christians Be Nuclear Pacifists?' *GrassRoots* reprint (Celebration Services [Post Green] Ltd.)

Lind, Millard. *Yahweh is a Warrior* (Herald Press, 1980).

Litherland, Alan. *A Short Guide to Disarmament* (Housman's, 1982).

McMahan, Jeff. *British Nuclear Weapons, For and Against* (Junction Books Ltd., 1981).

Merritt, Sandy. *Peaceworking* (United Nations Association, 1982).

Merton, Thomas. *New Seeds of Contemplation* (New Directions, 1972).

Merton, Thomas. *On Peace* (Mowbrays, 1976).

Myrdal, Alva. *The Game of Disarmament* (Spokesman, 1980).

Neild, Robert. *How To Make Up Your Mind About The Bomb* (André Deutsch, 1981).

New Statesman papers on destruction and disarmament: *Britain and the Bomb (New Statesman Report 3).*

Palme, Olof. *Common Security: A Programme for Disarmament* (Pan, 1982).

Publishing Committee for Children of Hiroshima. *Children of Hiroshima* (1980).

Radical Statistics Nuclear Disarmament Group. *The Nuclear Numbers Game: Understanding the Statistics Behind the Bomb* (RSND, 1982).

Rogers, Paul; Malcolm Dando, and Peter van den Dungen. *As Lambs To The Slaughter* (Arrow, 1981).

Ruston, Roger. *Nuclear Deterrence – Right or Wrong?* (Catholic Information Service, 1981).

Sampson, Anthony. *The Arms Bazaar* (Hodder and Stoughton, 1977; Coronet, 1978).

Schell, Jonathan. *The Fate of the Earth* (Picador, 1982).

Scott, Gavin. *How to Get Rid of the Bomb* (Fontana, 1982).

Sider, Ronald J. *Christ and Violence* (Lion Publishing, 1980).

SIPRI. *The Arms Race and Arms Control* (Stockholm International Peace Research Institute/ Taylor and Francis, 1982).

Sivard, Ruth. *World Military and Social Expenditures* (World Priorities, 1982).

Smith, Dan. *The Defence of the Realm in the 1980's* (Croom Helm, 1980).

Sojourners magazine and Sojourners Peace Ministry. *A Matter of Faith* (Sojourners, 1981).

Stein, Walter, ed. *Nuclear Weapons and Christian Conscience* (Merlin Press, 1961/1981).

Thompson, E. P. and Dan Smith, editors. *Protest*

and Survive (Penguin, 1981).

Working Party of the Board for Social Responsibility of the Church of England. *The Church and the Bomb* (Hodder and Stoughton, 1982).

Yoder, John H. *Nevertheless: A Meditation on the Varieties and Shortcomings of Religious Pacifism* (Herald Press, 1971).

Yoder, John H. *The Politics of Jesus* (Eerdmans, 1972).